© 1997

Mad about Mead!

Catch the Madness

Bring out that brewpot and get bubbling! On a brilliant autumn day, revel in the taste of "Howling Jack"—a honey-pumpkin mead the color of a ripe peach, with the smoky bouquet of autumn leaves. Got the sniffles? Bring on the Honey Mint Brandy, based on a traditional recipe that kept our Colonial ancestors warm and sneeze-free. When you want a robust brew for a cold January evening, drink an earthy mead that symbolizes hibernation: rhizamel, made from root vegetables, fruit and honey! Or raise a toast to spring's fertility with a glass of dandelion metheglin or "Honeysuckle Heaven": both delicate and fragrant as a patch of spring violets after a rainshower.

Mad About Mead will instill all your meadmaking with fun, creativity and magic. Enjoy the finest ambrosia that fruit, flower and honeybee can fashion. All you need is this book, a kitchen, and some good friends to toast in celebration!

About the Author

Pamela Spence holds a degree in English with a minor in philosophy from the Pontifical College Josephinum, Columbus, Ohio. Course work in commercial beekeeping at Ohio State University, however, led to a chronic bout with "bee fever," an obsessive passion about honeybees for which there is no known or desired cure. In 1986, she founded the American Mead Association (AMA) to stimulate interest in an alternative market for honey. The association, through its publications, the *Meadmakers' Journal* and *Mead Letters*, served as a clearinghouse of information for amateur and commercial meadmakers worldwide.

Spence has contributed articles on beekeeping and meadmaking to the *Llewellyn Organic Gardening Almanac* and various beekeeping and wine trade publications. During her tenure as AMA director, she conducted numerous workshops, lectures, tastings, and mead judgings. In addition to her mead activities, she is also a poet and storyteller, and currently lives on the banks of a creek in Central Ohio with her luthier husband and their family of children, dogs, and bees.

To Write to the Author

If you would like to contact the author or would like more information about this book, please write to her in care of Llewellyn Worldwide. We cannot guarantee every letter will be answered, but all will be forwarded. Please write to:

Pamela Spence
c/o Llewellyn Worldwide
P.O. Box 64383, Dept. K683-1
St. Paul, MN 55164-0383 U.S.A.

Please enclose a self-addressed, stamped envelope for reply or $1.00 to cover costs. If outside the U.S.A., please enclose an international postal reply coupon.

Mad about Mead!

Nectar of the Gods

Pamela Spence

1997
Llewellyn Publications
St. Paul, Minnesota 55164-0383
U.S.A.

Cover design: Anne Marie Garrison
Interior illustrations: Kathy Kruger
Photo on page 93: Pamela Spence
Photos in chapter 7: Lisa Novak
Editing and book design: Amy Rost

FIRST EDITION
First Printing

Library of Congress Cataloging In-Publication Data Pending
ISBN: 1-56718-683-1

The untitled poem by Psyche Torok (page 30) and "Making Mead" by Michael Sisson (page 41) appear with their respective permission.

The equipment shown in the photos in chapter 7 appears courtesy of Northern Brewers homebrewing store (St. Paul, Minnesota).

Publisher's Note

Llewellyn Worldwide does not participate in, endorse, or have any authority or responsibility concerning private business transactions between our authors and the public.

All mail addressed to the author is forwarded but the publisher cannot, unless specifically instructed by the author, give out an address or phone number.

The publisher has not tested the recipes included in this book and takes no position on the effectiveness or accuracy of the procedures.

Llewellyn Publications
A Division of Llewellyn Worldwide, Ltd.
P.O. Box 64383
St. Paul, MN 55164-0383, U.S.A.

ORDERED: MON. 4-16-01
REC'D. WED. 4-18-01

PURCHASED: PHONE ORDERED: "RENAISSANCE Catalog Magazine" FALL 2000
P 12.95
A 12.95 + $1⁰⁰ EXPIRES 4-30-01
T 13.95 SHIP ADDRESS: CHIVALRY SPORTS, Inc. PHONE = 1-800-730-5464
P.O.Box 18904, TUCSON, AZ 85731-8904

$\mathcal{D}$edication

To the Moonspinners of Columbus,
and to the memory of Susanne Price (1968–1996),
a meadmaker who truly served the gods.

NOTE: I WAS ORDERING SOME VERY EXCITING BOOKS FROM "RENAISSANCE CATALOG", AND DECIDED ON A WHIM TO INCLUDE THIS BOOK IN THE ORDER. FROM THE BLURB IN THE CATALOG I EXPECTED VERY LITTLE; NOT MUCH; VAGUELY SATISFYING TO MY MINISCULE CURIOSITY ABOUT MEAD.

TO MY SURPRISE & DELIGHT ⟶ PART I PAGES 3-38 IS ABSOLUTELY FASCINATING !!! AND CAREFULLY EXCERPTED PASSAGES WILL BE WONDERFUL ADDITIONS TO MY COLLECTION OF INFO ABOUT BEES.

THE SECOND PART OF THE SURPRISE WAS THE THE "VERY EXCITING BOOKS" THAT WERE THE (REAL) CATALOG ORDER TURNED OUT TO BE FIZZLES & DUDS!

ONE NEVER KNOWS, DOES ONE?

4-18-01

Contents

Recipes

Preface

MEAD—IT WAS THE DRINK of red-bearded Viking and sloe-eyed sorceress. It was already an ancient beverage when Aristotle drank it, already steeped in mythological mystery when Arthur toasted his Knights Templar. What role does mead play in our space-gazing, technological civilization? What relevance does the "back then" have to the "here and now"? Why bother making mead or seeking it out, when it is so easy to buy mass manufactured beverages in any convenience store? Indeed, why bother?

We live, so many of us, in a society divorced from the natural rhythms and cycles of life. Central heating has banished those long winter nights of campfires and hero tales; electric lights have driven demons from the dark corners and dimmed the magic of the midnight sky. But in spite of our clever inventions and gadgets, in spite of our arrogance and insulation, we are still human; still animal, organic, seeking, grieving, singing fools at play in the surf of the galactic ocean.

The story of mead is intertwined with the stories of humankind. Mead has been present at ritual, celebration, and remembrance down through the ages. Grapes, however, were found to ferment much more quickly and predictably than honey, and were far easier to gather. One didn't have to risk the wrath of bombastic bee to get the brew bubbling.

Over the course of centuries, humans domesticated the vine to their commercial advantage. In those regions that have enjoyed great benefit from the wine trade, however, mead is still brewed for sacramental use. People choose mead, seek out mead, honor mead precisely because it is not convenient, not everyday, not packed in Styrofoam and poured into a plastic cup. Mead comes to us with context intact, trailing streams of myth and ritual in its wake.

In the following pages you will find a smorgasbord of information. Consider me your tour guide as we set sail for a whirlwind tour of the land of milk and honey. As you will see, this dreamscape, this magical kingdom, has been with us humans all along, from the beginning of time—in our language, in our rituals, in our yearnings. In the first section we will visit many cultures and observe how they have translated a body of belief surrounding bees, honey, and mead into rituals associated with rites of passage.

In Part 2, we will look at how to make mead at home. Once we have mastered the basics, we can dive into Part 3, the section on mead and other recipes, and explore some options, expand our horizons.

Who knows, you might become an amazing meadmaker and desire to turn your avocation into vocation. If you want to sell mead, or any other alcoholic beverage, however, you must apply to Uncle Sam and all his little nephews to become a bonded winery or brewery first. Turn to Chapter 17 on commercial meadmaking and discover the emerging phenomenon of meaderies. You will learn firsthand from the trailblazers who have braved the paperwork jungle and survived, as well as a few war stories from those who did not. The Appendix, "Resources for Meadmakers," will enable you to find others who share in this mead madness or other kindred afflictions.

A lot of this book is concerned with making mead. But allow me to clarify here: this is a book that considers the many ways that people have made and continue to make mead. Meadmaking is not independent of the people who make it. Meadmakers are not necessarily like homebrewers or commercial winemakers, even though these latter groups may also make mead. As New Zealand meadmaker Leon Havill of Havill's Mazer Mead will readily tell you, meadmakers are "funny buggers." They take an oath long before birth, long before the stars learned to sing. They have methods and recipes entwined in their DNA, remembered deep in their souls. They will tell you: "I am a meadmaker; I serve the gods."

This book is unapologetically eclectic, geared to those who are intrigued by the idea of mead as well those who actually make it. It has been my experience that meadmakers share a fanatical devotion to mead but differ greatly in their approach and attitudes. I have, therefore, included the means and methods of real people—real meadmakers—that I encountered during my years as director of the American Mead Association. You will find directions for brewing pumpkin mead right in the pumpkin alongside laboratory-tested recipes for melomel; recipes that call for bee pollen and forage fruit alongside those that use commercial yeast energizers and acid blends.

Approach the information in this book as you would a street bazaar—a feast of experience, wisdom, and joy spread before you. Take what appeals to you, speaks to you, is relevant for you, and leave the rest. I had the privilege during my years as director of the Mead Association to encounter just about every way to make mead—scientifically, superstitiously, seriously, and foolishly. I know from conducting numerous workshops that some people break out in hives if you bring out a hydrometer but still manage to consistently make fabulous mead. I know of others for whom the sun rises and sets on lab analysis and whose mead tastes like crankcase oil. The opposite is also true, of course; no value judgment is intended here. As they say, the proof of the meadmaking is in the sampling. I have chosen to present you with a random sampling, therefore, warts and all. The ball is in your court.

Is this book exhaustive? I hope not; I have no desire to exhaust you. It is, rather, a sampling, a tasting of delectable morsels that abound in the land of milk and honey. There are many more books to be written, many more methods and perspectives to be explored. Consideration of mead-ale is not covered in this book, for instance, neither is the topic of sparkling mead or mead-champagne. Check the Appendix for other books on these topics.

Meadmaking should, above all, be fun, magical, mirthful. You don't have to be a laboratory rat or a techno-cat but a dash of the rakish adventurer doesn't hurt. I hope only that you will be inspired to read further, sample more widely, and treat more kindly the bees you encounter.

Blessed bees!

Acknowledgments

THERE ARE SO MANY PEOPLE who have been fellow travelers and tour guides on my own particular mead adventure that to thank them all would take a book in and of itself. Those I mention here are but a small percentage of the people who have been a part of the mead revival. To those who were there for the founding of the American Mead Association: Michael Sisson and Jack Kuehn, the Ohio State Beekeepers Association, the staff of Agricultural Technical Institute of the Ohio State University, particularly Dr. James Tew; the oenological staff at Ohio Agricultural Research and Development Center, particularly Drs. James Gallander, R. Reisen and Joe DelMasso; the Cornell University connection, especially Dr. Roger Morse and Bob Kime; Delaware

University's Dr. Dewey Caron; and Ohio Wine Producers Association director Donnie Winchell. I owe you all a debt of thanks.

Thanks also to the Homebrewers connection: Charlie Papazian of American Homebrewers Association and Byron Burch of Great Fermentations, Scott Francis of The Winemakers' Store; the Asair Mike Murray and Robert Stine Jr.; Jace Crouch and the Brewer's Guild for their recipes, encouragement and support; to all the commercial meadmakers including Frank Androczi of Little Hungary Farm Winery, the Oliver Family of Oliver's Winery, Khiron of As You Like It Meadery, Leon Havill of Havill's Mazer Mead, and everyone else who sent me a most welcome bottle of mead. Thanks are in order for the efforts of Susanne Price and Julian Strekal in carrying forward the vision of the American Mead Association. Susanne's untimely death left a deep void in the meadmaking world.

Thanks to *Gleanings in Bee Culture* editor Kim Flottem for his input on beekeeping matters; to Ben Slay for bee support; to Grace Firth for her inspiration and assistance with mead recipes; and to Michael Sisson and Psyche Torok for permission to use their poetry.

On a final note, heartfelt thanks go to my editor Amy Rost, whose wisdom and good cheer made the editing process more fun than is probably legal.

Above and beyond this small sampling of folks, however, I am indebted to the many, many meadmakers who have kept the art and craft and magic of meadmaking alive.

Part I

Milk and Honey in Myth and Ritual

Chapter 1

Background: Milk and Honey as Godstuff

FROM THE EARLIEST TIMES OF humankind, honey has been regarded as godstuff. While still in our evolutionary infancy, still thrashing around in the underbrush, hunting and grunting, we humans have believed that the sticky, golden sweet was a gift from the gods—dripping down from heaven to settle on tree and flower, whence it was gathered up by honeybees.

Honey was the only naturally occurring sugar in predawn civilization. When honey was removed from the beehive or bee colony, it fermented naturally. Fermented honey or mead is generally acknowledged to be the oldest alcoholic beverage known to humanity.

Every civilization that has had dealings with honey and bees—from the Amazon Basin to the Mediterranean coastline—had a variation of a basic core of belief: that honey originated in the dwelling place of the gods—"heaven"—and was therefore imbued with divine qualities. Additionally, honey bees, as earthly agents, enjoyed a special relationship to the gods. Possession of the magic mead signified divine authority among the Immortals and made them immortal. By consuming honey, humans were allowed a glimpse of eternity, a taste of the nectar of the gods.

The Land of Milk and Honey

If honey was understood to be the sacred fluid of heaven, milk signified the sacred fluid of Mother Earth. The ancient Celts, those great tree worshippers, used hazelnut milk to brew mead. In this way, they ritually reunited heaven and earth by combining milk and honey. This same notion informed early Christian baptismal rituals, as well. Initiates were given a drink of honey-sweetened milk, signifying the promise of paradise, the long lost land of milk and honey.

We humans, in all our diversity, nonetheless share a familiar image: a paradisiacal place we once inhabited but have now lost. Almost all mythologies and religions, practiced by everyone from the ancient desert Hebrew to the aboriginal bushman, contain the foundation myth that at some time in the past, gods and humans shared the same space and were on good terms. We recall that Hebrews had it made in the Garden of Eden and the "Golden Age" Greeks lived in the land of eternal spring and abundant food. Aboriginal bushmen gorged on an ever-yielding fruit tree and African villagers ate freely of the body of the great sky god. In every instance, the mortals eventually blew it. They became too greedy, too arrogant, or far too curious. By whatever transgression, mortal annoyed Immortal and was flung to Someplace Else.

The use of honey and milk in ritual anticipates the great day of reconciliation, a regaining of the land of milk and honey when all sins are forgiven, all injuries forgotten. The gates of Paradise will swing open, hostilities between male and female will be healed, mortal and Immortal will be one, heaven and earth will embrace. Honey in heaven, honey on earth—the golden thread connects us to that promised time still to come. Christians anticipate this as an "end-time," "up-in-heaven" sort of event. Newly Christianized Finns sang to the Virgin Mother as sky goddess, imploring her to send them honey from the heavens mixed with the milk of her heavenly breasts.[1] The rough and ribald Vikings had a similar idea. For Erik and Hrothgar, paradise was Valhalla, an endless party where mead flowed unceasingly from the teats of Odin's goat and was served up by the ultimate "milk vessels," the beautiful Valkyries.

Those of us who operate from a spiritual basis are guided by a similar personal belief: ultimate reunion with the Divine Source. We see our lives and changes as a process that moves us ever closer to that moment. The fact that honey is the crucial element keeping us connected to the Divine Source is evidenced by its widespread use in the rites of passage of many different cultures. Jarich Oosten, in his work *The War of the Gods: The Social Code in Indo-European Mythology*, maintains that the quest for mead and the magic cauldron is the single most important myth in the Indo-European culture. Anthropologist Claude Levi-Strauss, in his work *From Honey to Ashes*, documents a similar ritual importance of honey among the Amazon Basin natives.

All rites of passage, such as birth, baptism, puberty, marriage, and death, involve a "little death" and subsequent rebirth. Once the old role is surrendered, honey, imbued with divine, life-giving power, is the necessary food to bring forth the new, transformed life.

These rites typically involve two actions: eating and anointing. The initiate must "eat" the god—take the god into him- or herself (the Greek term for this is *ethenos*: the god within)—and the initiate must also be anointed by the community—publicly recognized as one of the faithful.

Bees as Heavenly Agents

The importance of honeybees as providers of this sacred food cannot be stressed enough. Almost universally, bees were understood to be agents of the Divine Ones. It is they that make the sacramental food for worship. Flowers produce nectar, but it is the bees and their spiffy enzymes that make nectar into honey.

Honeybees appear again and again in myth (most notably among the Indo-Europeans) as protectors of the Immortals, particularly the children. Rhea hid in the cave of sacred bees, for instance, for the birth of her son, Zeus. She left the infant concealed there to protect him from the child-devouring father, Kronos. In this place he was protected and fed by three sacred "nurse bees." Dionysus and Pan were similarly honey-fed infants, protected by the sacred *melissae* or bee priestesses. Later, human priestesses serving in the temples to Cybele, Artemis, and Demeter were commonly known as melissae, the Greek word for bee.

Bees as winged messengers also kept open the avenues of communication between the worlds. There is a core belief among many peoples, such as the Egyptians, Celts, and Anglo-Saxons, that the soul has the form of a bee and that when the person dies, the liberated bee-soul flies home to heaven. The ancient Egyptians believed that each human had a double or *ka* akin to a soul, and that this double went about in the form of a bee. When the individual died, the ka returned to Ra, the great sun god.

Scots in the Middle Ages likewise believed in bee-souls, but feared them as agents of darkness. Women accused of witchcraft were suspected of taking on the form bees to fly about and create their evil mischief.[2]

Northern Europeans believed that when a beekeeper died, the survivors must go to the bees to tell them of their master's death. "Telling the bees" was an important ritual to be followed in order to persuade the remaining bees to stay rather then to take wing and follow the master to heaven. A traditional rhyme is still recited in England:

> *Honey bees, honey bees hear what I say!*
> *Your Master, poor soul, has passed away.*
> *His sorrowful wife begs of you to stay,*
> *Gathering honey for many a day.*
> *Bees in the garden, hear what I say!*

Encoded in many of the folk tales of the Christianized Northern Europeans are stories that bespeak of the bees' favored status. In one Hungarian tale, the beginnings of the world featured three characters: God, the Devil, and the honeybee. God often dispatched the honeybee as a secret agent to gather information about the Devil's activities. On one such mission, the Devil discovered her, and as she attempted to fly away, he lashed her with his whip, severing her body. God healed her, of course, but it is because of this encounter that the honeybee has a characteristic segmented body.[3]

A similar tale explains how she got her stripes. In her role of undercover celestial agent, she was assigned to become helper and protector of humankind. It was believed that the bee, alone of all the animals, escaped from the Garden of Eden unchanged, except for her color. In Paradise, her coat was snowy white; the stripes on her back were the result of brushing past the burning sword of the angel who guarded the gates. Some say she was in such a rush to catch up to the departing humans; others suggest that it was done deliberately to provide her with believable camouflage. In any case, it became her duty to accompany these unfortunate ones into the world and provide for them the food of Paradise, the food that would eventually call them home.

An old Welsh law, in fact, requires that beeswax be present before the Mass is celebrated, in homage to the bee that left Paradise because of the sin of man.[4] According to a long-standing tradition among the Slavic peoples, eating honey on Holy Thursday (also known as Green Thursday) gave protection against the "sting" of a serpent.[5]

In the following chapters, we will see how important the use of honey is as we move through our rites of passage, from birth and baptism, through puberty and marriage, and as we make the final journey home. The sweet taste of honey restores our memories and keeps us moving ever onward toward that goal.

Chapter 2

Birth and Baptism Rituals

IN OUR MAIN-LINE, WESTERN MINDSET, we lump the celebrations of birth and baptism together. Often it is an official naming ceremony, wherein the lace-dressed infant is handed over to minister or priest for a ritual blessing with water. It was not always so, however.

Birth rituals were originally acknowledgment of physical birth and a guarantee of the child's right to life. Baptism, on the other hand, celebrated spiritual birth, a conscious choice made by one who had attained the age of reason and had received a "call." The difference between the two depended on the initiator. Birth rituals were performed on the child's behalf; they were an expression of blessing, protection, and welcome. Baptism was understood to be self-initiated, a pilgrim's quest.

Birth rituals mark the beginning of our human journey and therefore are of primary significance. Although we are only dimly aware of the fuss that is being made over us at the time, those who have participated in our creation and care are moved to celebrate. Historically, honey was a most significant element in birth ceremonies because it was understood to be the divine food, thus the life giver.

Typically, honey was smeared on the lips or shoved into the mouth of the bawling babe. In the belief system of the ancient Greeks, newborn babies were considered spirits—insubstantial, not yet authentically human. They believed that their goddess Helle took care of "spirit children" while such beings awaited birth into the physical realm. She gave them milk from an ever-flowing fountain, honey from eternally blooming flowers. This enchanted food nourished the unborn and kept them content. When children were first born they were still associated with Helle and could be sent back to her realm without sanction.

This belief provided the legal justification for a widely accepted practice in the pagan world, that of repudiating new-borns. Decisions as to the fate of the newly born usually resided with the father or an elder kinsman. Thus the adult in charge could choose to accept or repudiate the infant. The signifier was a sacramental meal of milk and honey. If the child were repudi-ated, it would not be fed. The unwanted child was either put to death directly or abandoned to die of exposure. Once the child had been fed the sacred foods, however, it could not be killed without consequence. Milk and honey were the foods that sig-naled transition from spirit to substance and the right of the child to exist in the world was recognized by all.

While rejecting the practice of repudiation, the upstart Christians integrated the pagan ritual of acceptance into their own rites of baptism. Barnabas, one of the earliest leaders of the Christian faith instructed his converts to administer the cup of milk and honey to all infants as a sign that the child is claimed henceforth as a child of God.[1]

Similarly, in Hindu tradition, the newborn child was blessed with a piece of gold (or golden spoon) then fed honey, milk, and butter while the father implored the gods to protect and ensure long life for the baby. Honey was considered to be the essence of life, pouring forth from the sun; milk and butter, of course, represented earth. Feeding the child this combination of foods represented the taking in of the All. It was done as an anticipatory gesture, anticipating reunion with the Divine at the end of physical life. We see again the expressed notion of physical life on this earth as preparation for the eternal afterlife. Birth rituals celebrate the arrival of one who has lately come from God. The child is like a visitor from home.

(**Warning:** Having painted this golden picture of the birth ritual, let me caution you against adopting such rituals for your own use. Neither honey nor cow's milk is considered safe food for an infant. Honey contains spores in suspension that can produce infant botulism; cow's milk contains all manner of things that play havoc with an infant's digestive tract. **Don't give either honey or milk to a baby.** Use milk and honey in birth celebrations by all means, but use the alternative practice of "waving the chalice over the infant" and have the adult participants actually drink the milk and honey or mead on junior's behalf.)

Baptismal ceremonies came later in life, when the initiate had received a sign or had been called to become part of a spiritual/religious community. For Native Americans, the call usually took the form of a dream and was specific to the individual;

among many hunting societies, such as the Amazon Basin natives, the first kill during a hunting season constituted a sign. Consuming honey in these rites was an act of welcoming the Divine into one's own physical body. The person became transformed, filled with the wonder and sweetness of God.

Initiates into many of the mystery cults, such as the Persian-based Mithraic cult, used milk and honey to drink a draught of the divine. The Mithraic cult, which became popular with Roman soldiers during the latter days of the Roman Empire, was based on worship of Mithras, the Persian sun god. Thus, the initiates were instructed to mix honey and milk, and drink it before sunrise. As their god rose in the sky, the initiates felt the warm glow of their god within.[2]

The ancient Hindu understanding of fermented honey or mead as a divine drink related to the element of fire is also based on an association of honey with the sun. Once again, the sun had a representation in divine form: the god Vishnu. It was believed that Vishnu had three footsteps in heaven and those steps comprised sunrise, zenith, and sunset. In each of these sun-steps sprung forth a fountain of mead. The Hindu initiates' use of intoxicating mead fortified their belief that it was a substance mixed from cloud vapor, imbued with the sun's fire, a gift from their god. Fire imagery was linked to the notion of purification, burning away obstructions so that limited human eye opened to the limitless vision of the Divine.

Baptism then, and everything that transpired during that rite was, in fact, a re-birthing process. The initiate was born again, recalled through the spirit as a child of the Divine. In early Byzantine Christian initiation ceremonies, the (adult) "newborn" was stripped, washed, and oiled by the priests. He was then wrapped in white robes and consecrated. The priests prepared three chalices: water, milk and honey, and wine. Water represented the God, the honeyed milk represented the Divine Child, recoverer of Paradise, and wine, not surprisingly, represented the Holy Spirit.[3]

This re-birthing, this return to innocence, echoes the birth ritual. In the former, the person is claimed physically; in the latter, the person is claimed spiritually. Although the elements are almost the same (milk and honey and the use of water), we now have the addition of wine—the fire element, the purifier. Children, either because they were believed to be in a state of perfect innocence or because they were not yet ready to engage the world, did not need "fire."

In the succeeding chapters, we will see how each rite of passage builds upon these basic elements and basic themes.

Chapter 3

Puberty Rituals

JUST AS BAPTISM AND BIRTH rituals have merged, or are sometimes aspects of the same ritual, baptism and puberty rituals often overlap. In some societies, an individual undertakes a spiritual quest, which we have previously seen as necessary for baptism, as part of his or her puberty rite. Likewise, in some traditions, puberty and marriage rites are elements of the same ritual. Ceremonies surrounding the onset of a girl's menarche might culminate with her marriage.

The onset of puberty is perhaps the most powerful, disturbing change we experience as humans. It is a time of individual, physical awakening, the coming into one's personal, procreative power. Becoming sexually mature or "ripe" gives us no end of

15

difficulty, particularly in our post-modern society. Adolescents in our culture often find themselves in limbo, physically mature but economically dependent; capable of reproducing but unable to provide adequately for a family.

In times past, such momentous transitions and all the conflicting emotions they inspired were dealt with through ritual. The young person went through a period of transition marked by:

1. **Isolation**—Removal from the social group, physical deprivation of food and shelter, confrontation of inner and outer "demons."

2. **Symbolic death**—Death of the child-self through surrender or ritual battle; transformation and initiation begin.

3. **Rebirth**—Transformation complete; return from the wilderness, ready to assume new roles and responsibilities.

At the conclusion of the rites, everyone acknowledged that the child was "dead." Having undergone the puberty rite, the celebrant was transformed into an adult. He or she assumed new duties, wore different clothing, perhaps moved into new quarters, or was given away in marriage.

A common theme in ancient puberty rites for both males and females was that of "acting the bear." This terminology was used by the ancient Greeks as well as among many tribes of Native Americans. The archtypical Bear was a powerful animal—literally and symbolically—and occupied a special place in the belief systems of many cultures: Viking, Celtic, Greek, Native American, and ancient Japanese, for example. Because this animal was observed to hibernate, reappearing magically out of the ground in the springtime, Bear became linked with the notion of immortality.

Added to this fact, of course, was the bear's fondness for the sacred food all immortal beings, honey.

Among the northern forest-dwelling cultures, Bear was considered to be the closest human relative, a kinship claimed by the jungle-dwelling natives of South America as well. "Whoever has met a bear in the forest knows that as soon as he sees us he stands up with a gesture of recognition and greeting," writes short story author Juan Jose Arreola. Arreola maintains that both Latin and Teutons claim the bear as family. "Let us confess: we have a common cave past with them."[1]

Anthropologist David Rockwell, in *Giving Voice to Bear*, notes that bears are considered universally to be a female symbol, regardless of the actual sex of the animal. In Native American traditions, for instance, the bear belonged to the domain of the Earth Mother and bear rituals were performed according to the phases of the moon.[2] The Great Bear Mother was immortal as interpreted symbolically through her annual hibernation and re-emergence. Often in spring, she appeared with cub, born in the womb of the Earth. This cub was believed to be an incarnation of the divine (male) child.

The Divine Son—Bear Cub—actually represented returning vegetation, the Green Man figure. Confusing though it may be, this is an important distinction: Mother Bear signified the Goddess, immortal mother of all animal life; Bear Cub was understood to be god of vegetation and must die to be reborn. This distinction figured into the differences between male and female "bear" puberty rights. When boys "acted the bear" they enacted Bear Cub, under the protection of the Bear Mother; when girls "acted the bear," however, they became the terrifying, destructive Bear Mother, the Mother-Destroyer.

Female Rites

√ Menstruating, unmarried girls were considered to be as dangerous and unpredictable as a she-bear. Ancient Greeks called these girls Brides of Death or *parthenos*. Girls were removed, isolated during puberty rites, as a protective measure for the greater community.

√ Greek puberty rites for young girls were associated with the goddess Artemis. Artemis is both the "Untamed One," virgin of the hunt, represented by the she-bear, and Ephesian Artemis the Great Mother, represented by the many-breasted bee-goddess. A primary feature of the Greek girls' puberty rites was participating in a dance to Artemis called *arkteuein* ("acting the bear").

√ No doubt those young girls had a great time acting the bear. During their isolation, they were allowed to be animals—wrestling and roughhousing, unconcerned with grooming or bathing, greedily devouring raw food, including honeycomb and bee larvae. At the conclusion of their bear time, the girls flocked to the dance. They whirled and spun furiously, dancing themselves into a state of near-exhaustion. Then, in the dramatic climax, they tore off their bearskin robes and finished the dance naked. The young girls acted out the virgin Artemis, the Artemis who fiercely vowed to remain a virgin, who ran free in the mountains with her dogs, attended by virgin nymphs; Artemis the strong and wild she-bear, who abhorred marriage and cities.

√ How did Artemis, the virgin, become Ephesian Artemis, the Great Mother? Some say it was because of the intervention—or meddling—of Aphrodite. Artemis fell victim to love and desire. The bear dance culminated with the girls tearing off their robes, discarding the virgin sheath of Artemis. Now they were ready to assume the role of Ephesian Artemis, the Great Mother, the many-breasted queen bee who never leaves her home again.

Once they actually began menarche (girls who participated in these rites were between the ages of five and eleven), they were married off as quickly as possible and sent to the safety of a male-dominated household. Here they would assume their rightful roles as wives and mothers. An unmarried, fertile female was disaster waiting to happen.

While Greek girls devoured honey as part of their rites, unmarried women were specifically prohibited from eating honey in some African tribal groups. The prevailing belief was that eating honey inflamed the woman and she become reckless and wanton—a dangerous combination, indeed. Among the Thonga in South Africa, the woman could not eat honey for a year following her marriage, or until the birth of her first child.[3] If she tasted honey prior to that time, she would, in all probability, make like the foraging (female) bees and take flight.

Free-ranging female bees owe their freedom to the "sacrificial virgin"—the queen bee. She and she alone is tied to the hive and carries out the reproductive function of the whole group. We can postulate that the taste of honey might make tempt the woman to be like the foraging bee, a free-roaming female forever.

In bear rites, as we have seen, the female is considered as dangerous as the she-bear. One of the chief dangers is the power of sexual attraction she now exerts over the male. Additionally, there is a whole body of myth and folklore about sexual liaisons between human females and male bears. Women are believed to possess a special relationship with bears, as Arreola again notes, "If women are involved, there is nothing to fear, since the bear has for them an age-old respect...no woman would refuse to give birth to a little bear cub."[3]

We have with us still, in erotic terminology, the description of a woman's vagina as the "honey pot." It is an irresistible lure for the bear. Anne Cameron, in her poem "A Bear Story," describes a male bear foraging in the night, looking for honey while the bees are at rest. He happens upon a woman, lying naked in the grass, who seduces him with her own brand of erotic honey.[4] Rockwell tells us that many of our mythological heroes were believed to have been born of woman, fathered by bear. Included in the list are Ulysses, Beowulf, and Norse heroes Hygelac and Grettir.[5]

Male Rites

As with the girls, boys' puberty rites were marked by isolation, initiation, and emergence. At the conclusion of these rites, the male was ready to assume his adult duties as hunter and warrior (life-taker) and husband and father (life-giver). In most cultures, these functions were linked; a man could not marry until he had completed his initiation and proved himself as a capable hunter.

In the pre-industrial civilizations we are considering, survival was dependent on belonging to a group, which could provide help with hunting, food-gathering, protection, procreation. The phenomenon of the nuclear family simply did not exist; community was everything. It was expected that during the puberty rites, the individual would experience enlightenment through visions and dreams. When this was accomplished, the tribal elders filled him in as to the "secrets" and expectations of his new role as an adult member of the group. Honey was often the vehicle by which visions took wing. Hallucinogens such as mushrooms and other psychoactive plants were preserved, mixed, and prepared with honey. The golden sweet stuff acted as a buffer against some of the more toxic and bitter compounds contained in the plants.

Honey, because of its supernatural origins, was also associated with superhuman strength and fertility, desirable traits for a maturing male. Sexual prowess was believed to be directly related to physical strength, a notion that has survived into modern times. There is a Scottish saying, for instance, that asserts the belief that mead-drinkers are every bit as strong as meat-eaters.[6]

As we have observed in the girls' rites, honey-eating bear rituals were pervasive in puberty rites. Among the Dakota tribe of southern Minnesota, a boy's initiation into manhood was also called "making a bear" and the ceremonies began only after the boy had had a significant dream, indicating his readiness.

> *Many Native American initiation ceremonies suggest that Indians associated initiation with hibernation.... Rituals varied, as did the myths supporting them, but a common pattern underlay the differences, and that pattern—prolonged isolation, fasting, symbolic death and rebirth—paralleled a bear in hibernation.*[7]

As is often the case, initiates in rites of passage had to eat honey and be anointed with it as well. Among the Andaman Islanders, for instance, ritualized eating and anointing was the solemn concluding ceremony in male puberty rites. The boys were fed sections of honeycomb by the chief while the elders rubbed them down with honey. The boys were then given individual honeycombs, which they had to eat without the use of their hands. Once this had been done, the chief anointed the boys' heads with honey and massaged it into their bodies. Elders took the boys away and bathed them (note the similarity here to the Coptic baptismal rites). As in other cultures, when the boys emerged, they were recognized as adults.[8]

Puberty rites for young men of the Ge tribes in central Brazil were in preparation for the next big step: becoming hunter/husbands. A Ge male was expected to become a provider for his wife's mother's family group. One of the first duties he would be expected to perform was to secure adequate honey to brew mead for all his mother-in-law's family. Advice from the male elders, therefore, included not only hunting wisdom but how to get along with one's mother-in-law and all her extended family and dependents. The prevailing norm that dictated most of the behavior for the Ge was discretion—the need to keep all things in balance. They took only what was needed and shared any unexpected bounty. Excessive hunting or food hoarding was considered to be the greatest conceivable evil.

For ancient Greek boys, puberty rituals focused on worship of a variety of fertility gods who inhabited the deep woods and open spaces. Included in this wild bunch are the lusty gods Priapus, Zeus' wild boy, Pan, and Orthanes ("the erect one").

Worship of Pan took place not in manmade buildings but deep in the forests, often in caves (dens). He was called "savior of the bees" and honeycomb, which, along with milk, honey, and lambs, were offered to this frolicsome god.

To bring offering of succulent honeycomb to Priapus, the urgent Greek lad had only to go out into the garden where statues of the fertile god presided over the voluptous earth. The use of garden scarecrows, in fact, is thought to be derived from this Greek religious practice, although the comical straw man would no doubt blush to meet his model: a red painted wooden statue with enormous, exposed phallus, graphically representing the awakening of male hormones.

The ancient Hebrews, by contrast, kept sexual excess under wraps. Since one of the patriarchs' major campaigns was to eliminate thedisruptive influence of Goddess-centered paganism among their people, permissive sexual behavior was a major no-no. Gayre points out that while early Hebrew Biblical writings refer metaphorically to the land of milk and honey, little mention is made of actual beekeeping activities at that time:

> *(I)t would seem that it was perhaps due to the rela-*
> *tionship of the bee and her produce to…Ashtoreth, as*
> *the Great Mother was called by them, which made it a*
> *matter of policy for the scribes to avoid reference as far*
> *as possible to a creature so involved in the ritual of a*
> *religion which they so heartily disliked.*[9]

It is small wonder that puberty rites are so pointedly ignored in our culture. Within the Judeo-Christian framework that many of us have been steeped in, sexual awakening represents chaos—a dangerous, destructive force that, when unleashed, brings about our downfall. In the foundation myth (as it has come down to us) of the Garden of Eden, we have been told that it was through disobedience and subsequent sexual awakening that humans got kicked out of the Garden. This sexual awareness brought about the alienation of man and God, and man and woman.

Eve is usually seen as the major transgressor, the devil's pawn. Not only did she disobey, but she also dragged hapless Adam along with her. Some commentators maintain that Adam had no choice, that her sexual allure was so powerful, he was unable to resist. Ancient Greek philosopher Philo saw this moment as the real "Fall" when the physical senses triumphed over reason, carnal over spiritual; when the man's desire for physical union with woman eclipsed his desire for spiritual union with God.

According to Islamic and early Jewish tradition, wine played a decisive role in weakening Adam's will. The only possible wine that would have been available in the Garden of Eden was mead. Recall that Eden was a place of no toil, hence no agriculture. Honey is the only sugar source that would ferment spontaneously, producing an alcoholic drink—mead.

Adam's nightmares have apparently been passeddown through the generations as a deep-seated fear of the seductive/destructive female. C. S. Lewis, in his autobiography *Surprised by Joy,* was none too joyful about his childhood nightmares and a resulting phobia about insects, among other things. "...(I)n the hive...we see fully realized the two things that some of us most dread for our own species—the dominance of the female and the dominance of the collective."[10]

The dominance of the female: the power to lead the male astray, to ensnare him and enslave him, arises out of the woman's all-powerful sexual allure. The male simply cannot resist; she has the upper hand.

Puberty rites, male and female, were preparation for the compelling urge to merge, to be fruitful and multiply. Female power in this arena eclipsed all other considerations: all the symbolism and traditions we have considered are in agreement. We are bombarded with recurring female, Mother Goddess imagery: She-bear, the moon, the temptress.

We will see in the next section how marriage ceremonies are meant to channel this powerful, potentially destructive force. Sexual awakening must be followed up as soon as possible by marriage. The female must be domesticated, and the use of mead in marriage ceremonies can be understood as an instrument of that domestication. Her powers at full throttle, the female eats the wild, sacred food—raw honey in the comb. In marriage, however, she is offered the transformed honey, fermented mead. Intoxicated, her defenses down, she can be easily overpowered and captured.

Chapter 4

√ # Marriage Rituals

MEAD HAS BEEN A INTERTWINED with wedding ceremonies since before recorded time. In many cultures today, mead is still the required ceremonial brew when couples tie the knot. In Ethiopia, for instance, which has no shortage of vineyards or grape wine, wedding guests toast the couple with *t'ej*, an African mead, a tradition which has been traced back at least as far as the fourth century.

If rites of puberty have been suppressed in our guilty body society, rites of marriage, by contrast, are writ large. Just ask the parents of any young bride. Young women of varying sexual experience still flock to the altar swathed in virginal white, their faces modestly veiled.

Modern males, often uncomfortable in this rush to public ritual, retreat to their own ritual: the bachelor party. We could draw a contemporary parallel here, of "acting the bear." Men (and increasingly, women as well) are encouraged to indulge their untamed "animal natures" one last time through ritual drunkenness and sexual display, safely removed from the domesticating influence of the impending marriage.

Among the Ge in the Amazon basin, marriage marked the end of the male puberty/hunting rites. Having successfully proved themselves to the other males through hunting prowess, the initiates were readied for marriage. Marriage of the new hunters was a collective affair. Prospective grooms were dragged from their huts or "dens" then led on ropes by their future mothers-in-law in a jubilant parade through the village. The bride's mother and family were no doubt savoring the notion of strong mead brewed from honey brought home by the hunters. As we have mentioned prior, one of the primary duties for the new son-in-law was to provide sufficient honey to make mead for all of the bride's mother's family.[1]

The great epic poem of the Finns, the "Kalevala," describes the mead-rich wedding ceremony of hero Ilmarinen and the beautiful Maiden of Pohjola. The maiden had chosen Ilmarinen, the handsome young smith, over the older, steadfast suitor, Vainamoinen, Son of the Wind: "...an old man is a nuisance/And an aged man would vex me." She indicated her chosen one by pouring him out a generous serving of mead.[2]

Golden-haired Celtic goddess Niamh, daughter of the god Manamman, had an appetite for beautiful young men as well. Choosing the legendary poet, honey-tongued Ossian, as her mate, she carried him off on her fairy steed, promising him life and love immortal in the mead-rich western isle, the Celtic Paradise. She kept him there, marinating in mead, eternally young and poetic. All was bliss for a few centuries until he became home-sick for his companions. Weary of his complaints, Niamh strapped him to her fairy steed and sent him back east for a visit, warning him not to set foot on the earth. Unfortunately, as he arrived in the Emerald Isle, the strap broke, dumping him to earth. Time caught up with him instantly and the beautiful young poet crumbled to dust. The honeymoon ended abruptly.[3]

Honeymoon, a term that we are all familiar with, is a specific reference to mead. The term comes from an old English tradition that dates from the Middle Ages. Mead was drunk in great quan-tities at weddings, and after the ceremony nuptial couples were given a month's supply of mead—sufficient for one full cycle of the moon. It was believed that by faithfully drinking mead for that first month, the woman would "bear fruit" and a child would be born within the year. If, indeed, the woman conceived, success was attributed to the skill of the meadmaker. The ability to produce life, that divine power, was believed to be imparted through the indulgence of the gods who gave humans access to the dew of heaven: honey, for their mead.

The production of this powerful elixir, this drink of life, was often governed by strict ritual behavior. In many cultures, par-ticularly in Africa, meadmaking was undertaken by people observing vows of chastity. The Masai, for instance, chose one man and one woman to make the mead. For two days prior and for the six-day duration of active brewing, the brewers were required to refrain from sexual activity. Breaking this vow was believed to result in the bees absconding (flying away) and the mead spoiling.

In some cultures, among the Ethiopians as well as among the Vikings, women were the primary meadmakers. Ethiopian girls learned the craft from their mothers and female relations, a tra-dition that survives today:

In Ethiopia, T'ej is made in private homes for family consumption…. Each household has its own family recipe…(and) the taste (of the finished mead) can be as individual as the imagination of the person making it. The same recipe can vary from mother to daughter, for the mead is made from instinct as much as from a recipe.[4]

Among the Albanian gypsies and many other ethnic groups of Central and Eastern Europe, blessing a couple's house with honey was common. Wedding guests, or the bride herself, smeared honey on the doorposts, gateposts, and window sills to keep malevolent spirits and mischief-makers at bay. Wedding guests then smeared honey on the doorway once the bride had entered the house. She might also be fed honey from a spoon by her mother-in-law, mimicking infant birthing rituals discussed in Chapter 2. Another widespread custom was that of smearing the bride's face with honey. Depending on the culture, the woman's eyes, mouth, or brow might be so anointed. This practice was followed in India and Africa, as well as among the Central Europeans.

These rituals were female-specific; they were done either by the bride or to her. Superficially, these traditions have been interpreted as ensuring sweetness and harmony in the marriage. Because of their similarity to ancient rituals involving the gods, and because they are gender bound, however, we can extrapolate a more primal meaning. In ancient Egypt, temple priests performed a ritual called "Opening the Mouth," which was enacted daily at the temple of Amen-Ra. Honey was smeared on the eyes and mouth of the idol and his mouth ritually opened to receive honey, the divine food. In hieroglyphic text, bee represents ka, the soul, which is brought into being in the physical world by the sacred food, honey. "The bees, giving him protection, they make him to exist."[5]

By anointing the bride in the same manner as anointing statues of the gods, the importance of her role in the ongoing process of procreation was sanctified. Because it was expected that she would bring forth life, she became momentarily godlike. Marriage was a precondition for this sacrament, of course. Both elements must be present and in harmony—male and female, mortal and immortal—for creation to continue. Anointing the nuptial house was the same action as anointing the temple. Before engaging in the holy act of creation, the participation and protection of the gods needed to be invoked.

Mead (fermented honey) played a starring role in wedding celebrations throughout Indo-European derived cultures. Fermented grain (cakes or breads), however, shared the spotlight equally with mead. Milk and honey are the sacred foods of birth and baptism, in celebration of the divine-child aspect. Bread and wine, on the other hand, produced when the basic foods are transformed by fermentation (the catalyst, yeast, is necessary for both), represents the mature aspect of divinity—creation. The wedding feast is thus symbolic consummation.

Milk, the female symbol, and honey, the male symbol, are to be found in the other—one contains the seed of the other. They must find and reclaim that hidden seed in each other for creation to continue. In discussing puberty rites, we made mention of the symbolic reference of female secretions as "honey." In erotic parlance, we find a mirror image of male "milk"—ejaculate. Psyche Torok uses this image in her untitled poem:

You, your hair flowing
  like a field of stars
beautiful young man
  unknowable as the dark moon,
I paint the dark moon
  on your brow
and search
beneath the folds of cloth
and clustered sheets
  ah, there
the guarded mystery
spilling over me and
filling the night
  like a meteor fire
  like your galaxy-hair,
the flow of the milky way.[6]

Wedding rites recognize the union of individuals and the expectation that they will continue the work of perpetuating the species. Survival of the species, a type of collective immortality, however, depends ultimately on the continued fertility of the land.

Vikings, who were well known as longship raiders, were, as well, agriculturists whose day-to-day survival depended on the fertility of their crops and herds. Women made mead and served it at the great feasts, mirroring the role of the mythical Valkyries, the givers of eternal life in Valhalla. Every spring, women prepared a mead offering for the sun god Frey, patron of springtime, fertility, rain, crops, sensual delights, and weddings. On the first day of plowing, village women carried brimming bowls of mead to the fields. A third of the bowl was poured into the maw of the open furrow, another third sprinkled over the back of the draught animal, and the final third was quaffed by the farmer himself.[7] Once again, we have the eating/anointing actions engaged.

The English tradition of wassailing apple trees on Twelfth Night performs a similar function and survives to this day in parts of Somerset and Devon. The purpose of the ritual was to charm the trees and ensure a good crop for the following season. The wassail bowl was filled with hot cyser (a honey-cider concoction) and roasted crab apples. Some of the steaming liquid was poured directly onto the tree roots. A piece of toast was soaked in the wassail and placed in the fork of the tree as well—the familiar sacraments of bread and wine.

These agricultural-based rituals celebrated the fertilization of earth with the sacred fluid of heaven. The sacred marriage ceremony was enacted each spring, as the earth awakened to her damp, fertile season. Honeybees played Cupid, gathering honey for the intoxicating mead cup, a covenant of love.

When the act of creation has been completed, nothing remains but the slow downhill slide to death. In the bee world, the male bee or drone has one and only one function: to fertilize a queen. Once this has been accomplished, the drone dies. In fact, in the process of mating, his sexual organ is torn from his body and he bleeds to death. Luckily, our processes are less dramatic.

Chapter 5

Death Rituals

W‍E HAVE SEEN HOW HONEY was revered as the foodstuff of immortality. Through the ever-repeating cycles of birth, death, and rebirth we participate in the never-ending pattern. Every major change in the human condition, which we celebrate through rites of passage, recognizes the necessity of death before the new phase can begin. The caterpillar has to die so that the butterfly may fly. Just as honey ritually signals the entry into life in this realm, so too does it signal the exit.

The possibility of death was never far from the minds of our ancestors. It is only in our modern era that we live with the consumer-driven delusion that we can halt the passage of time and ultimately cheat death. We buy "anti-aging" products that promise to rejuvenate our skins, our sagging bodies, and our drooping libidos. The closer we creep to the brink of planetary annihilation, the more we obsess about cellulite. The planet may blow up, but at least we'll go with smooth thighs.

Tribal peoples knew absolutely that a well-placed blow from a bear, lion, or spear could send them packing into the netherworld. They were humble in the world, recognizing the awesome power of life or death inherent in the caprice of winds, rains, and heaving earth. These peoples had no delusion of control when it came to environmental shakes and shudders, life and death. For the most part, however, they did have an unshakable belief in being part of a greater pattern. Death was a piece of the pattern, something beyond the horizon, something mysterious and magical. They prepared for death very carefully, with great ceremony, whenever the shadow of death hovered near.

For the Viking male, death in battle was the highest honor. As he set out for battle, therefore, he was fully prepared to die. Custom dictated that an offering of mead be poured out onto the waters as the longship tossed and strained at anchor in the wine-dark sea. This ritual was observed by Greek hero Jason, as well, who offered mead to the waters before setting off in search of the Golden Fleece.

The Aztecs believed that special rewards awaited men who had died bravely in battle and women who had died either in childbirth or as sacrificial virgins. These select few went directly to the House of the Sun. Not only were these golden souls permitted to accompany the sun as it made its appointed rounds, they were also offered the opportunity to become hummingbirds and feast on honey for all eternity. A sweet life indeed![1]

The Celts, always great believers in the powers of mead, poured out massive offerings before wading into battle. These outpourings most often went into the mead horn and down the Celtic gullet which did not always prove to be a prudent activity:

> *The sixth-century Welsh bard Aneurin relates the story of the battle of Cattraeth, in which Caradawg, one of King Arthur's battle-knights was killed. The army of heroes had feasted all night long, until at dawn they marched forth, "filled with mead and drink," only to be slaughtered by their enemies. Of Caradawg, the poet sang, "After the clear mead was put into his hand, he saw no more the hill of his father. Pale mead was their liquor, but it proved their poison...though pleasant to the taste, a fatal foe."* [2]

Although ever ready for death, these wild and woolly warriors anticipated victory. Their gods, after all, loved nothing better than a good fight and welcomed any opportunity to incarnate into a warrior body. Through the medium of mead, the companions issued the invitation for the gods to take them over and join the fray. Heroes were believed to be possessed by the war gods during battle, causing them to fight tirelessly, regardless of the wounds they suffered.

A key component of the Celtic (and Viking) front line were the "berserkers" (again, literally, *ber* means bear; *serk* means skin), an elite and fanatical corps of fighters. History tells us that these warriors played havoc with the highly disciplined Roman legions. It was rumored that the pagan priests primed the warriors on mead, then whipped them up into a fighting frenzy.

The Druidic priests drew heavily on the Celtic belief in rebirth (symbolized by identification with Bear) to quell fears about death. It has been suggested, additionally, that ritual drinking of mead was accompanied by the ingestion of psychoactive mushrooms, which rendered the warriors oblivious to physical pain, and ready to fight to the death.

On the battlefield, bodies of warriors were abandoned where they fell, left for the cold efficiency of carrion-eating birds. Once the flesh was ripped apart, the soul was free to pass over into the Otherworld. All the possessions of the deceased were similarly broken and mutilated, so that the essence or "soul" of swords, cauldrons, and drinking horns would be freed to rise up for the Big Party in the Sky:

> *It was the Celtic custom to bury important persons with everything they would need for a great feast once they reached the Otherworld. The Hochdorf tomb, dated at around 550 B.C. contained a huge bronze cauldron with a capacity of 104 gallons... inside the cauldron there was an ornate gold drinking bowl, or mazer, and a "powdery brown mass," identified as the dried remains of mead.*[3]

The ancient Egyptians, like the Celts, believed that this life was nothing more than a dress rehearsal for a better, more enduring life ahead. Nearly all Egyptian religious rites were concerned with the afterlife. The Egyptian practice of mummification stemmed from the belief that in the next world the dead needed their bodies, well preserved, as well as other worldly goods.

Before the body was mummified, priests removed organs from the body and preserved them in earthen jars. The jars were then placed around the body, in each of the four cardinal directions. Safekeeping of the soul was the particular responsibility of Horus' sons who were symbolized in hieroglyphics as honeybees. Horus was the overseer for souls while they were housed in physical bodies. He maintained soul vitality by means of honey, the divine food, which was dispensed by his sons. Nonetheless, the soul's overriding desire was reunion with Ra, the great sun god:

This god crieth out to their souls...and there are heard
the voices of those who are shut in this circle which are
like the hum of many bees of honey when their souls
cry out to Ra.[4]

Egyptian priests, the Kher-heb, ritually changed the foods left as offerings to the dead through chants and obligations. Priest and relatives then sacramentally "ate" the divine foods. To ensure that the dead could make use of the food offering, priests also performed the ritual of "Opening the Mouth" on mummies, just as they did on statues of the gods.

In Bulgaria, observations of All Souls Day, the Day of Mourning, required that the dead be fed a sacrificial meal. Candles and offerings of wheat and honey were placed on graves. The ritual foods were then offered to passersby with the words "May God forgive your sins." This custom was observed up until the twentieth century.[5]

The Egyptians codified into their religion the notion of care and preservation of the soul through the medium of honey. The Greeks, Assyrians, and Babylonians, however, used honey not only for its divine association, but also for its pragmatic, preserving properties. Alexander the Great died on campaign far from his homeland. His dying request was that he be sealed up in honey and carried home for burial. Honey made his request possible. This sweet treat keeps bacteria at bay, which is why it has been used for centuries as a wound dressing. Alexander's corpse would have been unwelcome cargo indeed without the powerful intercession of honey.

When Greek superhero Ulysses needed the prophetic vision of Teiresias (who, unfortunately, was already dead) to float his boat back to Ithaca, the enchantress Circe showed him how to make the only acceptable offering with which to gain entry into the underworld.

...we walked along the shore until we came to the place which Circe had described...I poured out the drink-offering for All Souls, first with honey and milk, then with fine wine and the third time with water....[6]

You will remember that these three offerings are the same ones used in early baptismal ceremonies; this time, however, the order of the offerings is reversed. This factor is one often encountered in magic: the "spell" or charm done exactly in reverse manifests the opposite effect. Baptismal offerings of water, wine, and milk and honey called the soul into the world to begin its journey with the body. The same offerings in reverse called the soul back home, to reunion with the Divine Source, when that journey was complete.

What Now?

Now our whirlwind tour through the land of milk and honey is complete. So many cultures! So many beliefs and rituals! And believe me, you've only had the briefest of introductions. You've discovered that all of your ancestors—as well as everyone else's ancestors—used honey and mead to anoint, consecrate, consummate, and inebriate. If you are not using honey or mead on a regular basis, you now know that you have been missing something really important in your life.

The cultures that have made mead have fermented it in jaguar hides, calabash gourds, goatskins, and earthenware crocks. You don't have to wear a white coat and peer at graduated cylinders to make mead (unless you really want to). The meadmaking adventure awaits. Turn the page and begin.

Part 2

Making Mead

Making Mead

First collect your materials. Honey:
the neon messages of corolla colors
flash like advertisements in a language absolutely
material, the sap secreted in the center
of buckwheat, clover, goldenrod—the names
allude to pastoral origins, essential
experiences, reality, that of which
we can not speak: a summer meadow
populous with blossoms and bees. Mix
it all up: honey and water, yeast
and the chemicals: sodium bisulfite, ammonium
nitrate: the latest last words from Western
civilization. Read some good books for the rest:
pounds to the gallon, days of fermentation,
myths and gifts of eloquence for the bards.

Put it in a quiet corner—no bright lights,
no barking dogs—let it work, froth and foam
and smell like unspeakable natural processes.
Siphon the good liquor off the top into a clean
carboy: each time you rack it there's a draft
to taste: the first is too rough, too cloudy,
too smoky, too yeasty, too sour, too wordy,
redolent of its raw sources: many rackings, many drafts,
always leaving behind the lees,
and finally when it's clear as a simple declarative
sentence, when one glass can make you hear humming
of wildflowering fields, put your mead in a bottle.
Cork it, age it, give it a name. Honey is
the bees' poetry: this wine is mine.

—Michael Sisson

Chapter 6

Meadmaking: A User-Friendly Overview

MAKING MEAD IS A LOT like making love; there's no "right" way to do it. In other words, meadmaking is as much an art as a science. The experience is different for everyone, and getting there is half the fun!

This section of the book will give you a clear idea of how to make mead. If you are the new kid on the brewing block, you will be happy to discover information on equipment and procedures, as well as plenty of practical hints. This first chapter gives you an overview of meadmaking equipment and processes, and translates brewing "techno-babble" into English. If you have ventured out onto the fermentation freeway previously, you will no doubt already be familiar with the concepts discussed here and the equipment described in the next chapter. In this case, feel free to flip around and peruse this section to find the information you need.

We define mead, in broad terms, as any alcoholic beverage that uses honey as the primary fermenting sugar. Honey and water are basic to the process. We humans have thrown wine yeasts and nutrients into the pot in an attempt to improve our chances of a bonnie brew.

Mead is produced when honey, the primary sugar source, is diluted down to a concentration that will support yeast growth. The diluted mixture—honey combined with water—is called **must**. This must is combined with activated yeast in a container called the **primary fermenter**. Once activated, the yeast consumes the sugar and gives off alcohol as a by-product; this process is known as fermentation. The activity of the yeasties can be encouraged and enhanced by the addition of various nutrients so they don't fall down on the job prematurely. In the initial stages, fermentation is impressive. Great masses of froth and foam arise, looking very much like fluffy lamb's wool. After about a week, the foam recedes and the liquid is then siphoned off or **racked** into a **secondary fermenter**. This second stage of fermentation can take anywhere from six weeks to

must: *honey and water mixture, combined with yeast.*

primary fermenter: *a container in which the initial, vigorous fermentation takes place; may be open or closed.*

racking: *process by which the must is siphoned off the sediment.*

secondary fermenter: *a container in which subsequent fermentation takes place; usually closed.*

a year or longer. The mead in progress is usually racked off the sediment once a month. When fermentation is complete and the mead clears—naturally or with a little help from the friendly meadmaker—then it is siphoned off into bottles, corked, aged to the appropriate level of maturity (mead and/or human), and consumed with great enthusiasm.

"What does it taste like?" you may be asking yourself. Because it is made from honey, many people assume that it must be sweet, but this is not always the case. It is said that Atilla the Hun was so unpleasant because he favored drinking unsweetened mead. Other people think immediately of Vikings and assume that it must taste like a hairy brown ale. In fact, depending on the materials and method, mead can be a frothing, foaming ale, a delicate table wine, or a full-bodied liqueur.

Strictly speaking, mead is made from honey, water, yeast, and nutrients. **Additives**, such as acid and tannin, enhance the fermentation process and affect the final balance of the finished mead. Adding fruits, flowers, herbs, spices, or other **adjuncts** produces mead variations, such as melomel (fruit), metheglin (herbs or spices), or mead-ale (grain). However, honey is the engine that moves the mead machine. How the

additives: *materials added to the must to enhance the fermentation process.*

adjuncts: *materials added to the must to enhance the flavor or the finished mead.*

vehicle looks, however, whether it can be compared to a Buick, a Bronco, or a Volkswagen bus, is up to you. You are the meadmaker; you rule the creation.

Over the centuries, humans have developed means, methods, and materials for making mead, which can greatly help or hinder the meadmaking process. Although every attempt has been made to present the material in a simple and straightforward fashion, depending on your experience or inclination, you may still have questions. Read through everything first. If you encounter terms, equipment, or procedures that you are unfamiliar with, flip to Chapter 7, Chapter 9, or the glossary for further clarification.

The Birth of a Legend: Just Do It!

This is a summary of what you do when you make mead using an open fermenter system. Everything summarized here is expanded and explained in the rest of Part 2—so relax and read on! Whenever you work with a mead recipe, however, you will be following this basic procedure with minor adjustments. If you find yourself confused or overwhelmed by any recipe, either in this book or from another source, refer back to this process. It is really not as hard as it seems. It is, after all, a very natural process.

In the Beginning: Conception

Day 1

1. Sterilize all equipment.

2. Sterilize the must (honey/water mixture) by heat or chemical means. (See Chapter 8.)

3. Prepare a yeast starter. (See Chapter 8.)

Day 2

1. Pour must into a primary —open—fermenter.

The golden virgin is ready.

2. Introduce yeast starter.

Fertilize!

3. Swirl, stir, or shake
   vigorously.

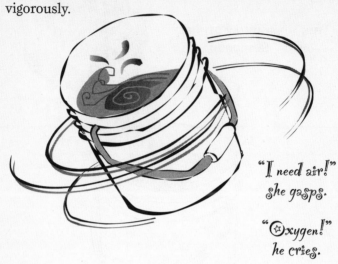

"I need air!"
she gasps.

"Oxygen!"
he cries.

4. Cover the entire fermenter loosely
   with plastic trash bag or a cloth.

A little
privacy, please.

𝒟ay 3-8 *(or thereabouts)*

1. Skim surface foam daily with a tea strainer.

What's a nice mead like you doing hanging around with this scum?

2. Speak words of encouragement.

3. Remember to re-cover the bucket each time.

Repeat these steps until the vigorous activity slows and the foam begins to recede, usually after the fifth day (more or less).

Day 8

1. Sterilize *glass* secondary fermenter, rubber stopper, air lock, and siphon hose.

2. Siphon must from the bucket into the secondary fermenter, leaving behind the sediment.

We be movin' downtown, Honey — leavin' that mess behind!

3. Top up the must with good water (bottled spring or mineral water).

4. Fit the bottle with the drilled rubber stopper.

5. Fill the air lock
   half full of
   water and fit
   into the
   stopper hole.

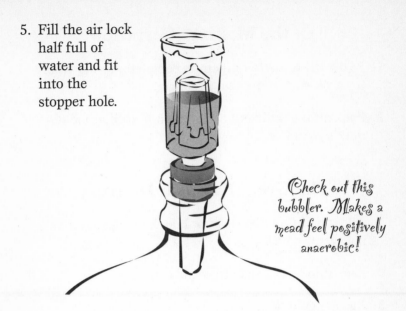

Check out this bubbler. Makes a mead feel positively anaerobic!

6. Place your fermenting
   vessel in a spot
   where it will not
   be disturbed or
   jostled for the
   duration.

In the Making: Gestation

1. Allow the mead to ferment to completion—anywhere from six weeks to a year or longer.

2. Rack off the sediment once a month until fermentation is complete.

The Great Reward: Delivery

1. Allow mead time to clear, or help it along with a fining agent.

2. Rack into sterilized bottles and cork.

3. Age to perfection.

Getting Started

Now that you have an overview of what is involved, the next chapters will discuss all the elements in more detail. Chapter 7, "Equipment: Tools of the Trade," will give you the lowdown on the "stuff"—containers, stirrers, measuring things—you need to make mead. The preparatory steps for "Day One" in above summary are elaborated on in Chapter 8, "Before the Recipe: Preparing Must and Starting Yeast."

Chapter 9, "Beyond the Basics," will help you get further acquainted with the primary ingredients and how they figure into the making of mead. After these steps, you will be ready to work with a basic mead recipe in Chapter 10, "Putting It All Together: Building a Mead Recipe."

Of course, after your first successful batch of mead, there is a good chance you'll have the itch to make more and different kinds of mead. Chapter 11, "Mead Variations," will take you to the exciting world of melomels, metheglins, and rhizomels.

Novice meadmakers often experience beginner's luck; your first batch is pure ambrosia. Sooner or later, however, you are bound to generate a grumpy grogg that refuses to cooperate. Chapter 12, "Problems and the Opportunity to Be Creative," should give you some guidance.

Some Words of Advice

Keep Accurate Records

This is the most basic piece of advice and the one that most people ignore. If you make a great batch, you will want to be able to duplicate your results; if your mead is undrinkable, you will want to have some idea as to what went wrong. Keep a fermentation notebook close at hand and note the date, recipe, specific measurements, procedure, temperature, and any other environmental factors or considerations. Make an updated entry every time you rack, noting any changes (measurable and/or speculative) in the fermenting mead. Your notebook will become an invaluable resource as you continue down that golden path of meadmaking.

Cultivate Patience

Meadmaking is not for those who seek instant gratification. The fermentation and aging process can take a long time. Brother Adam, the famous English meadmaking monk of Buckfast Abbey, ages his heather-honey mead seven years. Most meads mature and improve with age, so you will be investing a year or more in this process. You will, of course, take a small sampling at each racking to see how the brew is faring.

In the same vein, don't fidget over it. Leave the brew alone to work at its own pace. Don't move it or jostle it. Resist the temptation to pull the cork and sniff or sample. Every time you expose the brew to air, you risk contamination by airborne microorganisms which can spoil the mead. Rack once a month to get the mead off the sediment but otherwise, leave it alone.

Keep It Clean

Cleanliness is crucial to good winemaking. Sterilize everything that will come in contact with the mead—carboys, bottles, funnels, siphon hose, measuring spoons. At the same time, don't get obsessive; you are making mead, not performing open heart surgery. Let's not forget that there are cultures who have made and continue to make mighty fine mead in goat skins and gourds to no ill effect. Just use common sense and keep things as clean as possible.

Chapter 7

Tools of
the Trade

HAVING THE RIGHT EQUIPMENT IS basic to the meadmaking process. Luckily, most of the basic equipment is easy to find. There is some standard equipment, such as siphon hose or a scum skimmer (tea strainer), which you must have and which is available at any hardware or kitchen store. Then again, there is optional, specialized equipment, such as a hydrometer, which can only be purchased at a wine-supply store. Home wine and beer-making shops also carry the few specialty items, such as wine yeast and fermentation locks, that you will require. Many of these stores offer mail-order or e-mail service. What you need will depend in large measure on your style of meadmaking.

The Essentials

- Yeast starter bottle.

- Primary fermenter.

- Secondary fermenter.

- Siphon hose (clear plastic tubing).

- Rubber stopper.

- Air lock
  (also called a fermentation valve
  or bubbler).

- Sanitizing solution.

- Scum skimmer (tea strainer).

- Measuring spoons.

- Long-handled spoon.

- Bottle brushes.

- Funnel.

- Bottles, corks, or caps and corker/cappers.

Yeast Starter Bottles

Any small, long-necked, glass bottle that can be sterilized can be used to make a yeast starter. While some people prefer to use laboratory flasks, a long-necked beer bottle or individual-sized wine bottle will work just as well.

Be sure to use a container that is "food-grade" and has not been used for some other non-food purpose. See Chapter 8 for more on yeast starters and bottles.

Primary Fermenters

Primary fermenters are containers wherein the first vigorous stage of fermentation takes place, where the yeast is "pitched" (that is, introduced or thrown) into the must, and the game begins in earnest. Some people use a carboy (see the following page) or gallon jug, which is referred to as a closed fermenter system. (If you employ this method, be sure to allow sufficient air space in the bottle to accommodate vigorous foaming. Fill the container no more than two-thirds full.)

Others, myself included, prefer the open fermenter method. I find it preferable to carefully skim the foam daily—easy enough in an open fermenter—rather than allow it to build up in a carboy and express its enthusiasm all over the floor. Use a food-grade plastic bucket (honey buckets are ideal) or a newly purchased trash can (not the one you dump the coffee grounds in).

The must is fairly immune to contamination during this time of vigorous activity, because the yeast gives off carbon dioxide as a waste product. This gas forms a protective layer against oxygen and any hitchhiking microbes. The carbon dioxide is heavier than oxygen and exerts an upward pressure away from the surface of the must. Lightweight oxygen cannot overcome the pressure or penetrate the field of denser carbon dioxide molecules.

Cover the fermenter loosely with a sheet or plastic trash bag between skimmings, however, to keep out bugs, dust bunnies, and other miscellaneous household pets.

Carboys—Your Friends in Fermentation

A carboy is not the parking lot kid who squeals the tires of your new sports car. It is a big, glass jar that holds the fermenting brew. Think water cooler and you will get the picture.

Standard carboys.

Glass carboys hold anywhere from two and a half to eight gallons of liquid, are heavy and, obviously, glass. Glass has been known to break. Wise meadmakers tape up their glass carboys or place them in crates (wooden or plastic) for ease of movement. Commercial meadmaker Khiron from As You Like It Meadery discovered that plastic trash cans with their heavy-duty handles make ideal carboy holders and haulers.

Bottle brush.

Getting these boys clean can be a real challenge to your ingenuity and patience. You often end up with a murky-looking ring around the inside of the fermenter as well as sinister sediment that lurks on the bottom. An arsenal of long-handled bottle brushes is therefore essential.

Once again, keep your meadmaking brushes separate from the ones you use to clean out flower vases and aquariums. In the case of extreme crud (say you have inherited a carboy that had been used previously as a terrarium or ant farm) Arizona meadmaker Mike Murray suggests using sand. Pour in coarse-grained sand first, then replace it with progressively finer-grained sand until the container comes clean.

Secondary Fermenters, Rubber Stoppers, and Air Locks

After the first violent rush of activity, the must is siphoned into the secondary fermenter. These containers are narrow-mouthed because they must be stoppered with a drilled rubber stopper (available from the homebrew store) and fitted with a water-filled air lock (also known as a bubbler or fermentation valve). The fermenting brew continues to give off carbon dioxide but in greatly diminished amounts. Bubbles that rise to the surface of the fermenting must are the result of carbon dioxide activity. The air lock allows the brew to burp but not inhale; carbon dioxide escapes, but no oxygen gets in. Don't forget to put water in the air lock.

The secondary fermenter may be a gallon jug, a five- or six-gallon carboy, or a demi-john or jane. Whatever it is, make sure it is glass; the use of plastic here is beyond contempt. Plastic can interact with the developing mead in unexpected ways. One maker discovered he had lost an entire batch of raspberry melomel when acid in the must ate a small hole through the side of his container.

The other reason to use glass is that you can see directly what is happening to your baby brew. You can tell if a bacterial infection has taken hold, if it has ceased to throw sediment, or if it has simply changed color. You can marvel at it, speak words of encouragement, show it off to your friends.

Common air locks.
A bubbler (left) and a three-piece (right).

Siphon Hose

You get the must out of the primary fermenter and into the secondary fermenter by means of a siphon hose—a process known as racking. Do not simply pour the must from one container to the other; you will introduce too much oxygen into the liquid, creating a hospitable environment for that unwelcome microorganism Acetobacter (mother-of-vinegar). Use a length of clear plastic siphon hose, typically measuring five-sixteenths of an inch in diameter. Get enough to make life easy—three to eight feet, according to your needs. Place your secondary container below the level of the primary fermenter to benefit from the force of gravity. (See Chapter 10 for more details on racking.)

The purpose of racking is to get the must off the sediment. I know of at least one hapless meadmaker who attempted this by sucking up the sediment through a long tube. Although I understand he accomplished his goal, the experience was none too pleasant. Siphon off the clearing must and leave the gook behind rather than the other way around.

Sterilizing Solution

Sterilizing solution is available through your local homebrew store or can be whipped up in your kitchen using household bleach: two tablespoons to the gallon of water. Alternatively, you can boil the utensil in water and maintain the heat level for ten minutes.

Bottles and Caps

When all the hand-wringing, shouting, and weeping is over and the mead ready to bottle, you will need bottles. You can save and salvage wine and beer bottles, or you can buy new ones. The color and size of bottle is a matter of individual preference. A lot of meadmakers prefer clear glass simply because they like to show off the golden color of their mead. Commercially, most mead is bottled in clear, sloped-shouldered white-wine bottles rather than in the square-shouldered red-wine bottles.

Once the mead is in the bottle, it must be capped off. Some people do actually put their mead in screw-cap bottles but it is not recommended—certainly not by me. You will probably (at least, I hope you will) be aging your mead in the bottle for a year or so. You need a method of sealing that will keep oxygen and contaminants out of the mead. Use some type of bottle capper or corker. There are inexpensive hand-held varieties as well as heavy-duty floor models.

Handy Extras

There are a few other optional pieces of equipment that make meadmaking life easier.

- Racking cane.
- Bottle washer.
- Bottle filler or bottling cane.
- Wine thief (or turkey baster).
- Hydrometer and acid testing equipment.

Racking Cane

Since you will be racking the fermenting mead off the sediment many times—at least once a month—during the secondary fermentation process, save yourself much aggravation by using a racking cane. This cane is a rigid tube that fits down into the carboy. On the rubber cap that holds the cane in place is an outlet valve for the siphon hose. It has a "foot" and a perforated, bulbous end enabling you to siphon off the clear liquid and leave the sediment behind.

How do you get the siphon started? The same way you siphon gas out of a car: suck on the free end of the tube, get the flow going, then stick it down as far as possible into the empty container. To minimize excessive oxygenation resulting from happily splashing liquid, direct the flow gently down the sides of the glass. If you are concerned about contamination from your mouth when you suck on the hose, Colorado brewer Susanne Price has suggested taking a slug of high-grade vodka just prior to racking.

Refer to Chapter 10, page 93, to see a racking cane and siphon tube in action.

Bottle Washers and Bottle Fillers

Jace Crouch highly recommends the bottle washer, a brass gizmo that fits over the faucet and shoots a high-pressure spray of water into bottles. He considers it an invaluable time saver during bottling time.

Bottle fillers or bottling canes have shut-off valves that monitor the flow of mead into a bottle. I don't care to admit to the number of times I have sprayed mead all over my kitchen because I misjudged the rate of flow from carboy to bottle.

Wine Thief

A wine thief is a hollow tube inserted into the liquid to draw off a small sample of the golden brew. You can also use a (new) turkey baster, available in most grocery stores, for the same purpose.

Testing Equipment

Hydrometers, acid testing kits, and other such laboratory equipment can be helpful. By using them you can track measurable changes in the developing mead: acid levels, sugar concentration, projected alcohol level. You can measure, track, chart, graph, and compare a whole host of variables during the fermentation process.

At the same time, laboratory equipment is optional. Many home meadmakers rely on recipes, sensory evaluation, and instinct alone.

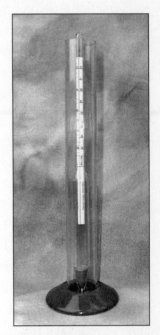

Hydrometer.
In a test tube.

More Extras: For Boilers and Brewers Only

- Brewpot.
- Candy thermometer.

As you will find out in the Chapter 8, there are two ways to sterilize the must before it goes in the primary fermenter—by boiling and by the addition of sulfites. If you boil you will need a brewpot and a candy thermometer; if you don't, you won't. If you are a lab rat, you will require testing equipment such as a hydrometer and acid testing kit. If you are a staunch "traditionalist" your sensory organs will suffice.

Brewpots

Brewpots that hold the must for boiling should be enamel, glass, or stainless steel. *Do not use aluminum*, as it can react unfavorably with the acids in honey. Many meadmakers favor enamel canning kettles because they have a large capacity, are relatively inexpensive, and are easy to find, especially around harvest time. Keep in mind that you will often be heating up four quarts or more of must at a time, so choose a BIG (mondo) pot. And please buy a pot specifically for meadmaking. Don't use the same pot you wash the cat in or dye your shoes in to make this ambrosia. Have some respect.

Candy Thermometers

If you are a brewer and heat your brew, you will need to keep close tabs on the temperature. A candy thermometer is indispensable for monitoring the internal temperature of the liquid. (See Chapter 8, "Before the Recipe: Preparing Must and Starting Yeast.")

Rule of Thumb for Equipment

The rule of thumb for any equipment, from measuring spoons to carboys, is to select utensils that are easily sterilized. A wooden mixing spoon is a lovely thing to behold but almost impossible to sterilize. Choose, therefore, plastic, glass, enamel, or stainless steel utensils. Purchase a special set for your meadmaking and use them only when making mead. If they become scratched and worn, replace them. Those dings and dents can harbor menacing microbes that muddle the mead.

Anything used as a container for the mead should be conducive to healthy, happy mead growth. I almost lost my cool entirely when one workshop attendee confessed that he had made his first batch of mead in a paint bucket "to see how it would turn out." For shame! Don't do it. If you are going to go to all the trouble of making mead, at least give it a chance of succeeding.

When making mead, think like a Boy Scout—be prepared. Assemble everything first, allow enough time to do the job properly, and by all means, know where you are going to put that five-gallon glass carboy for the next six months before you fill it.

Check out the options and choose according to your style and temperament. Don't be foolish and spend a lot of money on unnecessary gadgets. At the same time, don't be too proud; it is okay to make life easier on yourself. Just remember to have fun.

Chapter 8

Before the Recipe: Preparing Must and Starting Yeast

THE STEPS GIVEN FOR DAY One of the summarized meadmaking process (Chapter 6, page 44) are actually steps taken in preparation for carrying out the mead recipe.

Must Preparation: We Must Sterilize the Must—Or Must We?

Meadmakers sterilize the must—the initial mixture of honey and water—prior to introducing the "good" yeast, to kill off wild yeasts and other microorganisms that can spoil the developing mead. As discussed in greater detail in Chapter 9, "Beyond the Basics," naturally occurring yeasts in the honey are unstable and have a very low alcohol tolerance; they all die off when the mead reaches an alcohol level higher than 3 percent.

Option A: Better Living Through Chemistry

One way to sterilize the must is through the addition of sulfites. When you go to buy sulfites at the homebrew store, you will discover that they are available in a variety of forms and names. Thus, you can buy compounds such as sodium metabisulfite and potassium bisulfite, which are white powders, or Campden tablets, which are, obviously, tablets.

Wild yeasts go belly up in encounters with even small amounts of sulfites; wine yeasts, on the other hand, have a higher tolerance. Be aware that although their tolerance is higher they are not immune. Allow the must to stand approximately twelve hours after sulfite treatment before inoculating with wine yeast, or else the wine yeast will fall alongside his wild, osmophilic brother.

Procedure

1. Mix honey with water to make up total volume of recipe (1 gallon, 5 gallons, etc. See Chapter 10, "Putting It All Together: Building a Mead Recipe" for the correct proportions). Depending on whether you are using an open or closed fermentation system (and this is a matter of individual preference) you will be using either a food-grade bucket or a glass carboy. (See Chapter 10 for further discussion of these options.)

2. Add in acid, yeast energizer, tannin—everything except the yeast. You are now creating the must.

3. Add sulfite, either 2 crushed Campden tablets to the gallon or $1/3$ teaspoon sulfite per 5 gallons.

4. Mix, stir, shake it up, baby—aerate that must.

5. Allow to stand uncovered for 12–24 hours until the sulfur dioxide has evaporated.

6. Add the "good" (beer or wine) yeast starter.

Option B: Boil That Honey Down, Boys

Boiling the must accomplishes two primary things: it kills off the wild yeast spores (and any other undesirable microorganisms), and it bursts apart the protein molecules that can cause the stubborn "protein haze" of cloudy mead. Whether to boil or not to boil is a matter of individual preference. Some people who insist on "traditional" methods eschew any use of chemicals. Others boil for purely pragmatic reasons: it results in a quickly clearing mead.

How long to boil and at what temperature is one of those hotly contested topics that gets meadmakers foaming at the mouth. Part of the confusion stems from the fact that there are two considerations here: killing off wild yeast and bursting protein molecules. Many old recipes called for vigorous boiling of the must for thirty minutes or more. This method effectively breaks apart protein molecules, which results in a brilliantly clear mead. It should be noted, however, that boiling does not alter the physical structure of the component parts and occasionally the protein molecules recombine in solution. You may lay down a batch of perfectly clear mead in September only to find it has clouded up by June.

If your primary consideration is getting rid of protein haze, you will have to boil the must for at least thirty minutes. This is more appropriate for some of the darker, richer honeys that have a lot of particulate matter, such as pollen, suspended in them. In most cases, you will not want to boil light and delicate honeys, such as apple or orange blossom.

The major drawback to boiling is that what you gain in the eye, you lose in the nose; the bouquet or fragrance of the mead is all but destroyed. Enzymes in honey begin to break down in temperatures above 152 degrees. If your primary consideration is killing off the wild yeasts, rather than dealing with proteins (there are other methods of dealing with proteins later in the process), you might consider alternatives. The American Mead Association reports that according to new research by Ken Schramm and Dan McConnell, you need only heat the must to 145 degrees and maintain that temperature for twenty-two minutes to effectively kill off all wild yeasts. They indicate that this lower temperature will preserve much of the aroma, which is destroyed at higher heats.

Another popular method is the so-called flash pasteurization. Using this method, you bring the must up to a high temperature quickly, hold it there for a few minutes and then cool it back down abruptly. "…Sufficient pasteurization may be achieved in as little as one minute at 155 degrees F," according to Schramm and McConnell. Because of the precision required by this method, however, it is somewhat difficult for the average home meadmaker to achieve.

Procedure

1. In a glass, stainless steel, or enamel pan/brewpot (do not use aluminum as it may react adversely to the acids in the honey), dilute honey with a couple of quarts of water. You don't need to use the whole amount of water for this procedure. *Do* dilute the honey, however; honey tends to scorch and caramelize very quickly otherwise.

2. Add in acid, tannin, yeast energizer—everything except the yeast. (If you are making a melomel, do not add in *fruit* or *juice*; the pectin in the fruit will set and cloud the mead.)

3. Heat to desired temperature and maintain according to your purposes: 22 minutes at 145 degrees. for yeast extermination; 30 minutes at 155 degrees for clarification. Monitor temperature with a candy thermometer and *watch the pot*! If it boils over you will be scraping the sticky goo off your floor for ages.

4. Skim the rising froth with a tea strainer.

5. Remove from heat, cover, and allow to cool. This cooling-off process should be achieved as rapidly as possible; consider emptying out a refrigerator to accommodate your brewpot, sitting the pot out in the snow, or sitting it in an ice-water bath. The temperature must be between 75 and 80 degrees before introducing the yeast, or you will fry the little beastie's brains out.

Option C: Trust in the Universe

Although everything you read will tell you that you must sterilize the must, renowned scientist Dr. Roger Morse of Cornell University did a series of meadmaking experiments in which he
simply introduced the actively fermenting wine yeast into
unsterilized, undoctored must with no ill effect. Award-winning
English meadmaker Clara Furness reports similar results in her
book *Honey Wines and Beers*. "Since all of my winemaking
involved one of these methods of sterilisation, I tried fermenting
untreated musts with some trepidation, but I experienced no
failure. I now do this regularly...."

This particular method relies on the strength of the wine yeast
to quickly overrun the "home boys," producing a first wave of
alcohol that kills off the alcohol-intolerant osmophilic yeast.
Additionally, the carbon dioxide that is given off as a by-product
of the fermentation process provides an effective barrier against
any other airborne microbes. For this method to be effective, the
wine yeast must enter the arena at full fighting strength. A yeast
starter is crucial for this method, and highly recommended for all
other methods as well.

To Make a Yeast Starter

A yeast starter is a good idea regardless of the sterilization method
you use. Rather than throw a batch of sleepy yeast directly into
the maw of the must, awaken it gently in a small amount of fruit
juice. You will know within a few hours if you have a bad (dead)
batch of yeast without risking contamination of the entire volume
of must. (Note: Begin the yeast starter approximately twelve
hours before you expect to inoculate the must.)

Supplies

1   small, sterile, long-necked, empty, glass bottle.
    (Individual bottles that hold juice or wine work,
    as do laboratory cylinders.)

funnel

1   individual-sized can or bottle of fruit juice at room
    temperature. (The individual serving is sterilized
    before being sealed so you have a sterile medium
    in which to activate the yeast. For obvious reasons,
    don't use an already opened bottle of juice.)

1   packet wine yeast of your choice. (Note: beer
    yeasts tend to take off much quicker and more
    vigorously than wine yeasts. Use a bigger bottle
    and less time to prepare a beer yeast starter.)

sterile cotton

Procedure

1. Using a funnel, pour a
   small amount of fruit
   juice into the bottle (fill to
   no more than a third). Be
   careful not to allow any of
   the liquid touch the inside
   of the bottleneck, because
   the cotton stopper will
   wick up the wetness and
   open the highway to
   marauding microbes.

2. Still using the funnel,
    pour in the yeast. (Use
    a small amount of fruit
    juice to wash down any
    yeast cells clinging to the
    funnel.)

3. Swirl gently to aerate
    or introduce oxygen.

4. Stopper the bottle loosely with sterile cotton, put it someplace warm (in the sun or on the back of the stove), and let it work.

5. When the yeast is fermenting vigorously (usually within 12 hours), pour directly into the prepared, room-temperature must.

Having tenderly prepared your must and your yeast, you are now ready to start the basic mead recipe.

Chapter 9

Beyond the Basics

MANY PEOPLE MAKE FINE MEAD without knowing, or caring, about anything other than amount, time, and temperature. When I began making mead, I was mystified when one recipe called for tannin and another didn't; or when one meadmaker insisted on the importance of adjusting pH and the next three said it didn't matter. I began gnashing my teeth when I kept asking "why" and people would mutter some incoherent gibberish that made me suspect that they didn't know either.

This chapter is the result of my own blunders and subsequent pestering of smart people who seemed to know what it was all about. I kept at them until they put it in terms that even I could understand. Though much of this discussion is not absolutely essential for the making of mead, it might help you better understand meadmaking. Knowing why you are doing something gives you a better idea of how to handle problems when they arise and why not to do some things in the first place. Plus, understanding the roles of honey, yeast, acid, tannin, and nutrients in meadmaking will also help you build and perfect your own mead recipes.

Honey

To most modern consumers, honey is honey—the blended, pasteurized, bland honey found on the grocer's shelf. Commercial honey is blended down so as to be inoffensive to the average consumer's palate. In fact, honey is an amazingly complex sweet that, depending on the nectar source from which it is gathered, can vary in color from water white to an opaque black, with a corresponding intensity in taste. Some plants impart a characteristic taste and aroma to the honey. Honey from a mint field, for instance, has an unmistakable menthol taste. Orange blossom honey is less blatant, but still carries a slight citrus tang.

Honey is produced by the joint efforts of flowers and bees. Flowers produce nectar—a sticky, sweet substance, made primarily of sucrose—that the bees gather for food. They gather nectar, which provides them with carbohydrates, and pollen, which provides them with protein. Pollen is suspended in honey and strongly influences the final taste and color. Darker honey has a higher concentration of pollen, which can cause problems in mead if the protein precipitates, causing a "protein haze" (cloudy mead). Bees also add the enzyme invertase, which converts the sucrose into fructose and glucose.

When the moisture content of honey rises above 18 percent, honey will ferment because of the presence of naturally occurring osmophilic yeast spores. In the hive, bees keep the honey from fermenting by evaporating excess moisture. As the honey is unloaded into the cells of the honeycomb, house bees fan their wings rapidly until the honey is "ripened." Once the honey is at the correct moisture level, it is capped over with a thin layer of beeswax.

Once removed from the hive, however, the honey will ferment spontaneously if not properly stored. Because honey is hygroscopic, it will absorb water from the air. Once the moisture content increases, the dormant yeast spores become active and feast on nutrients contained in the pollen, larvae, and honeycomb.

Tasting honey will give you some indication of what to expect in the resulting mead. Check out a county or state fair beekeeping exhibit to see for yourself the range of honeys available in your area. Clover honey is popular for making a light-bodied table mead. Light honey also works well in combination with summer fruit for a refreshing melomel. Fuller-bodied honeys, such as basswood or nightshade, are desirable for rich sack meads. They also hold their own in combination with spices for metheglins or grains for mead-ales. Choose an appropriate honey for your recipe. By experimenting with different honeys you will find the type that serves you best.

Varietal honeys are honeys from a single nectar source (almond, fireweed, clover, apple, for instance). Beekeepers who harvest varietal honeys do so after the colony has worked a particular crop. Honeybees exhibit "plant fidelity," which means they gather nectar from primarily one type of plant at a time. Since the lifespan of a field bee during the summer nectar flow is about three weeks, she may only ever gather nectar from one nectar source during her entire lifetime.

Hives of honeybees are often rented out to pollinate a field crop, and the honey gathered at the end of a pollination assignment is likely to be largely varietal. The majority of beekeepers, however, take the honey crop off once or twice a season. They usually know what mix of plants the bees have worked. Spring and early summer wildflower honey tends to be lighter and milder than the pungent honey from the late-blooming flowers.

The best place to get varietal honey is from a local beekeeper. Actually, the best place to get any honey is from a local beekeeper (or become a beekeeper yourself). Contact your county extension agent or county bee inspector to find local beekeepers with honey to sell, or drive into the country and keep a lookout for those ubiquitous "Honey for Sale" signs.

Honey for market is either pasteurized or not. Honey is pasteurized—heated no higher than 160 degrees—so that it will flow through the filtration system more readily. This process does not necessarily kill off all the microorganisms present in the honey. Unpasteurized honey, also called "raw" honey, has received no heat treatment whatsoever. When honey is heated above 152 degrees, the aromatic enzymes begin to break down. For this reason, some meadmakers prefer untreated honey. Raw honey is sometimes referred to as "organic" honey, but this is not necessarily accurate.

Honey is a forage crop and therefore difficult to certify as organic. The purist definition of organic honey refers to honey that has been gathered from plants that have been grown without the use of pesticides or artificial fertilizers. The practical definition refers to honey that has not been treated with drugs or pesticides within the hive—honey from a hive that has not been treated with miticide, for instance. The bottom-line, pragmatic definition for organic honey, however, refers to honey that has not been heated above 160 degrees and has not been filtered through anything finer than a seventy-five-count mesh screen; at this level nothing smaller than legs and wings comes out.

Mead can be made dry or sweet, depending on the amount of honey used. Dry meads are made with two and a half to three pounds of honey per gallon of must. Sweet or sack meads are made with three to four pounds of honey per gallon. Too little honey produces a thin-bodied, low-alcohol mead that is prone to spoilage; too much honey can kill off the wine yeast, which cannot function in a high sugar solution.

The amount of sugar concentration in solution is measured by means of a hydrometer. The hydrometer reading will give you an indication of the potential alcohol content at completion. Hydrometer readings are, at best, approximate since the honey-water mixture will also contain miscellaneous matter that can affect the reading. The hydrometer is dropped into a cylinder filled with must. It will float at the point that its weight is displaced. Since alcohol is less dense than water, the greater the alcohol concentration, the deeper the hydrometer sinks. For a dry mead, you will want solution of approximately 22 percent honey to water, expressed as 1.095 specific gravity; for a sweet mead use 25 percent or greater, specific gravity 1.110.

Water

Would you buy a new Cadillac and fill it up with cheap gasoline? Would you serve hundred-dollar champagne in paper cups? Gad! If you are going to all the trouble of assembling the best ingredients for your meadmaking, *please* don't stop shy of the water. Use the best water available—spring water, bottled water (not distilled)—good quality water that doesn't smell like a swimming pool. Brother Adam, in his traditional approach to meadmaking, calls for the use of rainwater in the brew. Keep in mind that Brother Adam is now in his nineties. He has been brewing mead for a long time. I am sure that when he began making mead, acid rain didn't exist, as it does now. Rainwater in many parts of the country contains contaminants that you won't want in your mead.

Yeast

Yeast is a one-celled, living organism that, when unleashed in a hospitable environment, will consume the available food—in the case of mead, sugar—giving off ethyl alcohol and carbon dioxide as waste products. Naturally occurring osmophilic yeasts contained in honey are unstable and have a low alcohol tolerance. Most contemporary meadmakers choose not to rely on this yeast, but sterilize the must (see Chapter 8) and introduce a more reliable wine yeast. Wine yeasts commonly used in meadmaking are from the strain *Saccharomyces cerviseae*, variety *ellipsoideus*. Unlike the wild yeast which will die off in a solution of more than 3 percent alcohol, wine yeasts are active in concentrations of up to 14 percent alcohol.

Since yeast is a living organism, it is strongly affected by environmental stimuli, such as heat, light, noise, and vibration. For this reason, a working brew is often placed in a quiet, dark place where the temperature remains fairly constant. Many homebrewers, however (myself included), like to live close to their brews, infusing it with "hearth" energy. Thus, the working mead sits on a kitchen counter shrouded with quilts, or is tucked away safely behind the couch.

The optimum fermenting temperature is between 65 and 75 degrees. Too low a temperature causes the yeast to become inactive and cease fermentation; too high a temperature can kill off the yeast. The most desirable environment is one where the temperature remains relatively stable and does not fluctuate significantly.

There are a number of yeasts that have found favor with meadmakers; again, personal preference is the best guide. Experiment and use what works for you.

Types of Yeast

- **Champagne yeast** is a good all-around choice and the one most people start with (and many people stay with). It works in temperatures from 55 to 70 degrees and complements the flowery nature of mead. A moderately vigorous fermenter, it has a high alcohol and sulfur dioxide (SO_2) tolerance. This yeast, however, sometimes requires a longer period of aging to produce a good quality mead.

- **Montrachet yeast**, which ferments in temperatures of 65 to 80 degrees, works more vigorously and has a high alcohol and SO_2 tolerance. Some makers report that Montrachet has a tendency to impart a sulfuric taste to their mead. Others, however, report good results with it.

- **Prise de Mousse** will ferment your mead out to 14 to 15 percent alcohol if enough nutrients are present to maintain the fermentation. It is a vigorous fermenter that will remain active in cooler temperatures (down to the mid-40s) than some of the other yeasts.

- **Epernay 2**, by contrast, is the yeast of choice for a less alcoholic mead. It ferments best in temperatures between 55 to 75 degrees, and will produce mead with more of the fruit and floral tones intact.

- **Tokay** ferments best in higher temperatures (80 degrees and above) and is a vigorous fermenter. It tends to produce a mead with a more pronounced acid taste.

- **Wine yeast** is available in freeze-dried packets or in liquid form from wine supply stores. While a number of "mead yeasts" are available, mostly imported, they have not made a favorable showing with meadmakers in this country thus far.

Wine yeast gives the most consistent results in meadmaking. You should not rely on the wild yeasts, nor should you use bread or brewer's yeast. In spite of that piece of wisdom, people do. I know because I have talked to them. My question is always, "How did it taste?" More often than not, they tell me the mead was just fine and they drank it right down. If you do use one of these ragamuffin yeasts, at least try the wine yeasts in a batch or two to appreciate the difference.

Nutrients

Like most living things, yeast grows best when it is fed a balanced diet. Honey provides yeast with an abundant sugar source, which it uses as energy for growth. What honey lacks, however, particularly when the must is boiled, is nutrients in sufficient concentration, specifically nitrogen, phosphorus, and potassium. Winemaking supply stores sell prepackaged "yeast energizers," usually containing a combination of ammonium phosphate, urea, and cream of tartar. Non-chemical meadmakers favor primary source nutrients, such as raisins, bee pollen, or larvae.

The purpose of adding nutrients is to ensure efficient fermentation of the mead. Your goal is to get the yeast fermenting actively and to keep it working until fermentation is complete— until all the available sugar has been converted to alcohol. Without the nutrients, your mead will develop a "sugar high," an initial frenzy of activity that peters out prematurely, leaving the job half done. The fermentation process is more a cross-country race than a fifty-yard dash. Nutrients give the yeast stamina over the long haul.

Acid

The acid level of a solution is often expressed in terms of pH, the measurement of free hydrogen concentration in solution. Measuring the pH will tell you whether the solution is acid or basic, relative to a neutral point of pH 7. A pH reading of less than 7 is acid, more than 7 is basic. Honey has a pH of between 3 and 4, the same as grape juice. Honey, however, is a poorly buffered solution, containing only half as much acid as grape juice. When the honey is diluted with water for meadmaking, it becomes unstable—one might even say flighty. The hydrogen ions will eagerly hook up with any passing element, going for a joyride on the pH range. The addition of acid, like the love of a good woman, stabilizes the ions and keeps them from wandering.

If you want to check the pH of your must, you can purchase special pH paper that is color sensitive. After dipping the paper into the must, compare the color of the dampened paper with the color guide.

Acid is usually added to the must in the form of citrus peel, zest, or juice, or in the form of a packaged "acid blend," a crystallized powder containing a combination of 25 percent citric, 30 percent mallic, and 45 percent tartaric acids. Which form you use is a matter of preference; both methods have staunch supporters.

Meadmakers who pride themselves on making an organic or "all-natural" brew eschew using any form of powdered or prepackaged acid. It is their contention that using citrus peel (lemon, lime, orange, or tangerine) produces a cleaner, more flavorful, and aromatic mead. You have more leeway when using the fruit itself, simply because the acid is not in as concentrated a form as it is in the acid crystals. If you choose to use peel, scrub the fruit first to remove any pesticide or waxy residue. Use thin strips of peel, and a discrete squeeze of juice. While traditional wine-making texts indicate that high levels of oil from the fruit peel may retard fermentation, at the low levels we are discussing here, it should not cause any slowdown in the process. (Remember this point if you use citrus as a primary fruit in a melomel recipe.)

The importance in acid balance is most obvious in the finished mead. In sensory evaluation of wines, including mead, we are looking for a balanced product, neither too sweet nor too harsh. In tasting, sweetness is balanced by acid. A mead that is intended to be a dessert mead, with high residual sugar, needs more acid to avoid tasting cloying. There is no specifically stated sugar-acid ratio. It is more a matter of fine tuning, a matter of learned expectation. Too little acid produces a bland, lifeless mead; too much acid produces a sharp, harsh mead.

Our taste expectations grow out of a preconception—we often judge taste by comparison. Because of the prevalence of grape wine in our culture, we tend to judge taste by our "community standard"—our expectation of what a good wine should taste like. Many historical mead recipes yield very sweet, bland tasting meads. It is good to bear in mind that at the time the mead was being made, grape wine production was inconsistent; many of the wines were sweet and bland as well.

Testing for acid is done by means of a testing kit. The kits come with simple directions: to a measured sample of must, add a color solution. A neutralizer is added drop by drop (cc) until the color of the sample changes, then stabilizes. The number of cc's or drops of neutralizer that must be added to the sample to reach the stable color point indicates the percentage of acid present. Total acidity of the beginning must should read between 0.7 and 0.8 percent. Finished mead should have an acid level of between 0.5 and 0.7 percent because some acid is lost during fermentation.

Tannin

As with acid, tannin helps the brew work more efficiently and adds to the overall balance of the finished mead. Tannin binds the protein in honey and rides it out of solution. Protein binding is the most desirable method of clarifying mead since some of the other fining agents can have a deleterious effect on the taste of the finished mead. It has been suggested by a scientific meadmaking friend of mine that if you could determine the exact ratio of tannin to protein in solution, you should be able to consistently produce a completely clear mead purely through the action of the tannin. To my knowledge, no one has yet established that ratio.

Tannin affects the final mead by imparting an astringency, a mouth-puckering feel, that gives the mead some punch. In tasting, some people have difficulty differentiating between acidity and astringency. Simply put, acid stimulates saliva (the mouth waters); astringency produces the opposite effect, inhibiting saliva (the mouth feels dry).

Naturally occurring tannin is contained in black tea, stems, and leaves of plants and on some fruit skins. You can also buy prepackaged powdered tannin, usually derived from grape skins.

Not all recipes call for tannin. Recipes that call for hops, herbs, or fruits normally do not. Also, when using a light, delicate honey, you may choose not to add tannin.

Now that we have a handle on the basic ingredients of meadmaking, let's put them to work and get brewing.

Chapter 10

Putting It All Together: Building a Mead Recipe

I MUST CONFESS MY PREJUDICE—I am a purist. I came to mead-making from beekeeping and thus regard honey as the most perfect foodstuff on the face of the earth. My preference, therefore, is for a still, straight mead, redolent of honey, reminiscent of summer. I have tasted many metheglins and even more melomels, but the clean taste of an unadorned mead still thrills me. Melomels are the easiest to make and typically take the least amount of time to finish out. Additionally, it is possible to cover up a whole range of fermentation problems with herbs and spices, which accounts for the popularity of metheglins during the Middle Ages. You become a real meadmaker, however, when you produce your first straight golden mead.

From the following basic recipe, you can develop a working mead recipe that will be your most valuable resource and jumping-off point. As you gain experience in meadmaking, you will naturally make adjustments according to the taste and performance of the mead. Amounts listed here are approximate and intended as guidelines. Remember to keep notes in your fermentation notebook.

The Basic Building Blocks

- **Honey:** 2 $1/2$–4 pounds per gallon of water. The amount of honey you use will vary according to the style and strength of mead you are making.

- **Water:** Good water (spring or bottled); enough to make up to the total amount of the recipe.

- **Yeast:** 1 packet wine or ale yeast per 1–5 gallons of mead.

Using these three basic ingredients will enable you to make show mead. Show mead, made from these three ingredients exclusively, is the only mead eligible for competition at the London (U.K.) Honey Show.

Starting from a base of show mead you can tinker with additives and/or adjuncts. Additives enhance the working of the fermentation process while adjuncts affect the taste, color, or character of the final product. Technically, any time you add an adjunct, you have a mead variation rather than straight mead. We will consider these options in Chapter 11, "Mead Variations."

Remember, honey is the primary ingredient in mead and should never be used as an afterthought or mere flavoring. Variations should be built on a solid foundation of good meadmaking.

Use fruits or herbs only insofar as they enhance and complement the honey. Keep your priorities straight and consider honey first.

Additives

1. **Yeast nutrient or "energizer":** Equivalent of 1 teaspoon per gallon.

Honey, particularly when diluted, lacks sufficient nutrients to maintain healthy yeast activity. This problem is further exacerbated by boiling the must. Feed the yeast beasties so they can maintain sufficient energy for the long haul.

Alternate sources (per gallon of must):

- Raisins: a handful.

- Bee pollen: 1–5 tablespoons.

- Crushed bee larvae.

2. **Acid:** Equivalent of 1 teaspoon per gallon.

Alternate sources (per gallon of must):

- Juice and (one) peel of any citrus fruit.

- Other fruit juice, pulp, and skins.

3. **Tannin:** Equivalent of $1/4$ teaspoon per gallon.

Alternate sources:

- Brewed black tea: 1–2 tablespoons.

- Cream of tartar.

- Leaves, stems, and bark.

- Grape skins.

Note: Exact amounts of alternative additives will vary with the recipe and personal preference. Use the "equivalent" amounts as a rough guide, remembering that those amounts represent *concentrated* amounts, and that the amounts are *per gallon*.

"Chemical" vs. "Organic" Additives

People tend to toss these two terms around rather imprecisely. Because both words have strong emotional connotations it is worthwhile to clarify the situation.

"Chemical" additives are acid blends, tannins, yeast energizers, and other powders that can be purchased through a wine-supply store. These powdered crystals are synthetically derived.

"Natural" additives come from a primary source that contains the desired element. Strong black tea is a good source of tannin, for instance, just as bee pollen yields protein, a yeast energizer. Raisins contain nitrogen, and fruit peel and juice are added for the acid they contain. Needless to say, the natural additives may contain other substances as well. When adding citrus peel for acid, you also get a small amount of aromatic oil.

Please note that although some people refer to "natural" mead as "organic," this is not necessarily an accurate description. Unless the materials added to the mead are cultivated without the use of chemicals, the mead cannot truthfully be called organic.

"Natural" brewers will tell you that their method produces a cleaner, more aromatic mead that ages well. "Chemical" brewers will tell you that natural brewers are unscientific, sentimental purveyors of poppycock. At the judging table, both methods have won honors. So, make it natural, make it chemical, but whichever method you choose, make it mead.

Now that you have an idea of what elements go into the making of mead, let's look at a good working recipe.

Mead for All Seasons: A Basic Mead Recipe

This mead is appropriate for any season, ritual, or celebration. The recipe makes about five gallons.

Ingredients

16	pounds wildflower honey
4	teaspoons acid blend
6	teaspoons yeast nutrient
1	packet Epernay 2 yeast
1 1/2	teaspoon grape tannin
	good water to make five gallons

If the thought of chemicals makes you cringe, feel free to boil the must, substitute bee pollen for nutrient (5 tablespoons/gallon), strong brewed black tea for tannin (1 tablespoon/gallon), citrus peels (from 2–3 lemons or other fruit) for the acid blend.

Stage 1: Primary Fermentation

1. In a food-grade plastic bucket, mix honey with spring water sufficient to make 5 gallons of liquid.

2. Add $1/4$ teaspoon sodium metabisulphite and let stand for 24 hours (cover loosely with cloth or plastic sheet).

3. Stir in acid blend, tannin, and nutrients.

4. Add the yeast.

5. Swirl vigorously to aerate.

   At this point of the fermentation the activity of the
   yeast is aerobic—it requires oxygen to work. Be a
   shameless agitator and mix it up. Within a few hours,
   the brew will begin to work and froth vigorously.

6. Skim daily with a sterilized tea strainer.

   After a few days, fermentation will slow and the
   foam will recede.

Stage 2: Secondary Fermentation

7. Using a siphon hose, rack the must into a five-gallon
   carboy (leave any sediment behind) and fit with an
   air lock.

Leave only an inch or so of head space under the air lock to
reduce the amount of oxygen in the container. This stage of the
fermentation is anaerobic—carried out in an absence of oxygen.

Remember, because you will be racking your mead a number
of times before you are done, place the working brew high
enough to utilize gravity when racking into a new container.

Each time the must is racked, some of the liquid remains
behind with the sediment. Since excessive oxygen can spoil the
developing mead, you will want to minimize the amount of air
space in the fermenter. This can be accomplished by racking
into smaller containers. For instance, you may want to rack
from a five-gallon carboy into gallon jugs (as shown on the
opposite page). You can also mix a little extra must to begin
with, ferment the smaller batch in a separate container and use
it to top up the primary batch.

Racking mead.
During the secondary fermentation stage, the must is racked, in this case, from a five-gallon carboy into gallon jugs, using a racking cane and siphon hose. Placing the carboy higher than the jug lets gravity do the work.

Ideally, this stage of active fermentation will be complete within a reasonable amount of time—three to six weeks—but in some cases the mead will, in fact, continue to ferment for many months. Fermentation continues as long as the bubbles rise to the surface. (You will be able to see them.) You can also observe the escaping gas in the air lock. The frequency of the "glubs" in the water of the air lock indicates the vigor of the fermentation.

8. Rack the liquor off the sediment once a month during both active fermentation and subsequent clarification.

As the mead ferments, it throws off particulate matter; dead yeast cells, suspended proteins, and miscellaneous crud will settle on the bottom as sediment. Depending on about a zillion variables—type of honey, temperature, methodology, karma, phases of the moon, and just plain cussedness—the amount of sediment will vary. If your fermentation is atomic, there will be a landslide of sediment; if your fermentation is pedestrian, there will be only a modest amount of sediment. Typically, you will have the most sediment during that first turbulent month—typically, but not necessarily.

Rack the mead off the sediment once a month. Decomposing organic matter in the sediment can corrupt your impressionable young mead, leaving it with a unredemptive off-flavor and an unpleasant little spritz. As long as the bubbles keep bubbling, it is fermenting.

When all visible fermentation has ceased for at least a week, you assume that the fermentation is complete, unless, of course, you have a stuck fermentation. In the latter case, see Chapter 12, "Problems and the Opportunity to be Creative."

Stage 3: Bottling and Aging

9. When the mead is clear, rack into bottles, cork, and age for at least a year.

Rack the clearing mead off the sediment, replace the air lock and allow it to clear. How clear is clear? You should be able to read a newspaper through the lighter-colored meads and to clearly see the flame from a candle or match through the richer-

*Opaque: got a ways
to go yet.*

*Getting clearer, but
still not quite there.*

*Ah! Ready for
bottling, Sir!*

colored meads. When the mead throws no more sediment and is not hazy or cloudy, siphon into sterilized bottles and cork.

Allow the elixir to age in the bottle until it matures. Use individual serving-sized wine bottles as tasters to gauge the progress of your mead without having to sacrifice a whole bottle each time.

How long does it take to age? As long as it takes. The melomels and metheglins are usually ready after six months or a year, the straight meads may (but not necessarily) take longer.

Longing to Know How Long?

Everyone wants to know how long it takes before the mead completes fermentation, clears, and ages adequately. The first time I made a variation of Jace Crouch's Swamp Water Mead-Ale (see Chapter 14), it completed fermentation and cleared in six weeks. I was jubilant! Other more typical batches, however, have bubbled and murked for a year or more. I have made meads that hit their taste peak at eight months and declined rapidly thereafter.

However, most mead improves with age—anywhere from a year to five or seven years. There are so many variables—type of honey, temperature, yeast strain, pure cussedness—that no single answer will do. Enjoy the mystery and go with the flow. Fussing is futile and annoys the mead.

Expect vigorous activity in the initial stages of fermentation and resultant heavy deposits of sediment. Expect that the activity will gradually subside as time goes on. Expect to rack your mead once a month.

You have a right to expect these behaviors but not to demand them. Frank Androczi, winemaker at Little Hungary Farm Winery in West Virginia, leaves his mead on the sediment (or "lees") for the entire fermentation process. Just as the proof of the pudding is in the eating, the proof of the meadmaking is in the quaffing. Frank's mead is often killer.

Meads made from stronger honeys should improve with age. How do you know? You taste it from time to time. I have heard of people laying down an undrinkable batch of mead, forgetting about it for ten years, then discovering that it had evolved into a gem, much like a callow youth who manages to grow into a decent human being.

On the other hand, I've also suffered through tasting a twenty-year-old "gem" that smelled and tasted like death. Every mead has its peak. Once that peak is attained, there is nowhere to go except down. When it is good, drink it. And be sure to make some more.

Chapter 11

Mead Variations: Add an Adjunct or Two

WHEN YOU START ADDING ADJUNCTS—fruit, flowers, herbs and spices, vegetables, toad tongues, or whatever—you create a mead variation. Fruit and honey produces melomel; herbs and spices, metheglin; rose petals, rhodamel; vegetables, rhizamel. Outlined below are standard procedures for preparing the adjuncts. You can substitute and combine ingredients freely within these categories. Go ahead, get wild.

Melomels

Mash the fruit coarsely, pour the juice directly into the honey-water and suspend the pulp (in a muslin bag) in the must. Do not boil fruit or fruit juice as it will cause the pectin to "set" and cloud the mead. (If, for whatever reason, you do boil the fruit or juice, use a *pectin enzyme*, available at homebrew shops, to break down the pectin.) If you sterilize the must by boiling, add the fruit/juice after boiling, when the must has cooled.

Do not start primary fermentation of melomel in a closed fermenter, that is, in a glass carboy fitted with an air lock, as the fruit skins can clog the air vent and cause an explosion—**very dangerous**! Start the fermentation in the recommended open fermenter, a plastic bucket covered loosely with a sheet. After the primary fermentation is complete (five to ten days), rack the melomel off the bulk of the fruit.

Fruits often used in melomels include raspberries, plums, cherries, sloes, blueberries, cranberries, and citrus fruits. Mulberries produce a specific melomel known as *morat*, grapes yield *pyment*, pears and/or apples yield *cyser*.

Note: Choose your honey with care. Melomels are best made with lighter honey so as not to overwhelm the delicate flavor of the fruit.

Metheglins

It is very easy to overdo the gruit (the combined herbs and spices that make mead into metheglin). To guard against that tendency, some recipes suggest brewing an herbal "tea" first where you can adjust the strength and taste accordingly and simply add it to the mead at bottling time. Other recipes call for adding the gruit directly to the must. Eastern European tradition calls for boiling the must and gruit together then removing the herbs when the must has cooled. If you decide to add gruit directly to the brew, secure the ingredients in a muslin bag and suspend in the must. Allow it to steep no longer than twenty-four hours or else you may extract bitter elements from the plant material into the mead.

Some common ingredients for metheglins (either alone or in combination) are ginger root, cloves, nutmeg, vanilla beans, chili beans, coffee beans, walnut leaves, fennel, caraway seeds, anise, hops, and rosemary. You can get adventurous and experiment with anything that humans can safely eat and digest—seeds, roots, leaves, bark, flowers.

Warning: Use only those parts of the plant that are normally consumed. Pits and seeds from some fruits are toxic (peaches and plums, for instance). The use of wormwood, once used in the production of absinthe, is now illegal. When in doubt, refer to the generally regarded as safe (GRAS) listing. See the Appendix, "Resources for Meadmakers," for further information.

Rhodamel and Other Flower Meads

Technically, the use of flowers in meadmaking results in metheglin but since flowers require specialized treatment, we will consider them separately. Pick the blossom when it is full— in the case of roses for making rhodamel—just before the petals are ready to fall. Use only the petals; discard stems and calyx. Rinse in cool water and shake to dislodge insects. Pour boiling water over the petals, let stand one to four days (depending on the recipe and flower), strain, and discard the petals.

You can intensify the rose water by repeating the procedure several times, straining out the old petals and adding fresh ones to steep in the flower water until you achieve the desired color and taste. Traditionally, the petal and water infusion was placed in a sunny window to facilitate the process. Alternately, some makers use a handful of raspberries or strawberries in combination with red roses to achieve a pleasing red hue.

Some rhodamel recipes call for the addition of rosehips. Again, use only the "hip"; discard the calyx and stem. Slice and remove seeds. Mash coarsely, add to the petals and pour boiling water over the whole mixture.

Some flowers to try are roses, violets, elder flowers (sparingly! three to five heads is enough for a gallon), carnations, marigolds, dandelions, honeysuckle, and daisies.

Since some flowers are more intense than others, the amount of time required to extract taste and aroma will vary. Dandelions get funky if soaked more than twenty-four hours while the more delicate blossoms may take longer.

Rhizamels

Once again, technically, rhizamels could be considered metheglins, although others insist they are melomels. Since vegetables require special handling, we will consider them separately.

Scrub the unpeeled vegetables well and cut into small pieces. Place in a pan and cover with a gallon or more of water. Bring to a boil then simmer until the vegetables are tender but not mushy. Remove from heat, strain off the liquid, and discard the vegetables. Some recipes tell you to keep the vegetables swimming in the stew until the first racking. If you do this, treat the veggies as you would the fruit in melomels, and use an open fermenter to avoid the possibility of pulp or skin clogging the air lock. (Boom!)

Most rhizamels are made from root vegetables, including carrots, parsnips, beets, potatoes, or turnips. Get dirty and dig a veggie or two.

Chapter 12

Problems and the Opportunity to Be Creative

WELL, YES, IT DOES HAPPEN. You have followed directions, recorded, tested, and weighed. You have done everything precisely the same as when you made that last amazing batch of award-winning mead. In spite of all that, you find yourself gazing at a five-gallon jug of grumpy goo that refuses to bubble or brew. What has gone wrong?

It is a little-known fact that all fermentation is governed by the Cosmic Trickster, a mercurial mischief maker. This dratted prankster will see to it that your first few batches of brews are sublime, ambrosial. About your third or fourth time out, however, he just can't resist the temptation to meddle. He has to intercede and muddle your marvelous mead. He is as apt to appear in a 500-gallon fermentation vat as in a five-gallon carboy, as one of our commercial meadmaking acquaintances found out.

Meadmaking is an art—even when science is employed to enhance the process. Remind yourself that mead is made from honey and honey is a forage crop. Remind yourself that bees add the enzymes that make the nectar into honey. Don't forget about the yeast cells, either. As living organisms they have their own agenda. This is called the Litany of the Frustrated Fermenter. Relax, take a deep breath and let's see what can be done. If worse comes to worse, throw it out and start again. It isn't the end of the world.

Stuck Fermentation

When bubbles no longer rise to the surface of the brew, the fermentation should be complete—that is, all the available sugar has been converted into alcohol. Sometimes, however, the lack of activity is an indication of an incomplete or stuck fermentation. The yeast has quit working for one reason or other—it is too cold and the yeast has become dormant; there are insufficient nutrients to feed the yeast; or the yeast has turned belly-up and died for any one of a number of different reasons. You can determine whether or not the fermentation is stuck by taking a hydrometer reading or by sensory evaluation. A low-alcohol, overly sweet product will tell that the fermentation has ceased prematurely.

If the temperature in your fermentation chamber is too cold to support active fermentation (below 40 degrees, for instance) move the carboy, wrap it in an electric blanket, build a box with a light bulb in the bottom (a fermentation cupboard), or ship it to your uncle in southern California. Very often, even when the mead has cleared and does not appear to be throwing additional sediment, there may still be live yeast cells present, particularly if your carboy is sitting in a cool basement. In this case, before you bottle, move the carboy into a warm environment. (Now you know why you put it in some sort of carrying device, such as a plastic trash can, to begin with.) You may notice a secondary fermentation taking place—that is, the yeast begins working again.

Although some people will try to tell you that mead is supposed to be effervescent, don't believe it. Effervescence is evidence of a secondary fermentation (desirable only if you are making mead-ale, honey beer, or mead champagne, which is a whole other consideration). If you bottle prematurely, in regular corked wine bottles, chances are they will explode all over your basement. Although it happens to everyone at least once, avoid it if possible. There is nothing more frustrating than to find the fruits of your labors dripping from the light bulbs.

If the temperature is tropical but the bubbles are still not burping, you will have to reinoculate the must with fresh yeast starter. Remember to add an additional jolt of yeast nutrient as well.

If the mead is decently alcoholic—around 8 percent for instance—you can also attempt shock therapy. This method was recommended to me as a means of making fortified mead (technically illegal to do at home), but it also proved to be an effective means of salvaging an otherwise hopelessly stuck fermentation. I had racked a five-gallon batch of stuck mead back into an open fermenter in hopes of reviving it. When it did not respond I became quite annoyed and agitated. To teach it a lesson, I covered the bucket and turned the stubborn wretch out into the howling blizzard. I am ashamed to say that I set it out in the snow and promptly forgot about it.

When I rediscovered it—much later—the brew was covered with a thick layer of ice. In the middle, however, was a well of clear, potent, golden mead slush. I carefully dipped out the ice-distilled brew and toasted the arrival of spring. It was exquisite.

Cloudy Mead

As we have discussed previously, cloudy mead is caused by protein molecules suspended in solution. This is by far the most common problem in meadmaking, both for the home and commercial meadmaker. The fermentation is complete but the mead is still unappealingly murky. This is more likely to be a problem with darker honeys than light ones and more likely when the must has been sterilized by sulfites rather than by boiling.

One solution is to simply wait it out. In many cases the mead will clear naturally after a few weeks or months. You can sometimes speed the process along by subjecting the mead to a "cold break," that is, placing it in an extremely cold environment: out in the snow or in a refrigerator overnight. I have found this method effective in all but the most extreme cases.

If nothing works or if you are just plain impatient, a fining agent can be used to clarify mead. The traditional fining material is an egg white, lightly beaten in a small amount of the mead, then added to the big jug. One egg white will treat up to ten gallons of mead. From a winemaking store you can purchase a variety of fining agents such as sparkolloid (seaweed), bentonite (clay), or isinglass (sturgeon flotation solution). Allow the agents to do their work, then rack the clear mead off the sediment.

Yucky Mead

This is the ugly little glitch that no one likes to talk about. You can do everything right. The fermentation finishes out within a reasonable time, the mead clears, you bottle it, age it, taste it, and throw up. You have encountered factor x—in the service of the Cosmic Trickster, no doubt. Sometimes there is a reasonable explanation. Perhaps oxygen has insinuated itself and oxidized your mead into liquid rust.

Sometimes people overage the mead. They keep it around long after it has reached its peak and is now in a slow, ugly decline. Admittedly, this is not a common problem in our hurry-up age but it can happen. I have tasted some of these horrible, hoary meads. It is an experience about as pleasant as eating spider webs in a moldy pit.

Sometimes there is a taste suspiciously reminiscent of gasoline or crank-case oil. This off-taste can sometimes be traced to pollen in the honey. Not all pollen does this, mind you, just some pollens, in some circumstances.

I have also observed that particular honeys may be more or less problematic. There is one honey source, for instance, that has become notorious for making undrinkable mead. Our friend Jack first tipped me off to this fact. He had about twenty gallons of mead made from this particular honey. Since it tasted so dreadful after the first year, he stored it in his barn to let it age out. Every year he pulls out another bottle to see if it has mellowed. Every year it tastes as bad as the day he bottled it. Others have had similar experiences. I'm not going to tell you which honey it is (the last time I questioned the suitability of a particular honey for meadmaking, I was besieged by irate beekeepers and meadmakers alike). Just be aware that some honeys work better in meadmaking than others. That's all.

In the spirit of all the undaunted meadmakers of history, don't let the failures warp you. Keep good records, use common sense and don't weep over spoiled mead. If you've got room, let the stuff age; sometimes it will actually get better, sometimes it won't. You can always make more.

Part 3

A Cycle of Recipes

Chapter 13

Celebrating the Seasons:
A Sampling of Recipes

For everything there is a season,
and a time for every matter under heaven:
a time to be born and a time to die;
a time to plant, and a time to pluck up what
is planted…

Ecclesiastes 3:1

THIS SECTION CONTAINS A RANDOM sampling of recipes appropriate to the seasons with which to test your wings and venture into the adventure. The recipes include meads—which require fermentation paraphernalia—and other drinks requiring nothing more complex than a measuring cup. These are not hard and fast formulas; rather, they are recipes that I, or someone I trust, has actually used with good results. You're allowed to modify them. Honest.

If you have never made mead before, relax; it really isn't that difficult. Refer again to the basic mead recipe and procedure found in Chapter 6. The mead recipes in the following pages differ only in the ingredients and initial preparation. Once the must is racked into the secondary fermenter, the procedure is the same for all of them. I have therefore summarized the procedure in the recipes. (For your convenience, those recipes that are somewhat complicated or have special considerations have been broken into step-by-step directions.) If you forget what to do, refer back to the basic mead recipe.

In addition, with the authority vested in me, by me, I hereby give you permission to experiment and explore. Feel free to substitute lemon juice for acid blend, champagne yeast for Epernay, peaches for blueberries, a pinch more tannin, a smidgen less fennel. Get creative, get a little crazy, have fun, for heaven's sake. There are no hard and fast rules. One tiny suggestion, however— if you are whipping up a batch of truly bizarre mead (and people do all the time, believe me), make a small batch the first time. It can take a mighty long time to work your way through a skunk cabbage or newt nose mead.

If you really get rolling, there are now a respectable number of mead competitions at which you can test your talents (see the resources in the Appendix for details).

Bring out that brewpot and get bubbling!

Chapter 14

September Through December: Fall Harvest

THIS IS THE A TIME of harvesting and gathering in preparation for the long darkness of winter. In the hive, the female bees work diligently, cleaning out, consolidating resources, casting out the drones—those unfortunate sons and lovers who cannot pay their way—preparing the queen and now exclusively female colony for hibernation.

Meads

Cut Them Down Cyser
(Makes 1 gallon)

Apples, almost as much as honey, are big-name stars in mythology. Dispute over three golden apples struck the spark that eventually ignited the conflict that led to the Trojan War, which in turn caused the irreconcilable rift between gods and human. Likewise, in Judeo-Christian belief system, Eve's appetite for the Eden apple caused all kinds of trouble and left humans with a bellyache beyond belief.

Ingredients

1 1/2   pounds crab apples

3   pounds fall wildflower honey

1/2   teaspoon yeast nutrient
     (alternative: 5 tablespoons bee pollen)

1   tablespoon citric acid
   (alternaive: handful lemon peels)

2   Campden tablets

1   packet champagne yeast

   spring water enough to make up to one gallon

Procedure

1. Dissolve the honey in 1/2 gallon of water and set aside.

2. Mince apples and strain off juice into the primary fermenter.

3. Immediately add 2 crushed Campden tablets.

4. Add the honey-water mixture to the apple juice.

5. Add yeast nutrient and citric acid.

6. After 12 hours add the wine yeast.

7. Allow to work for about a week, skimming surface foam daily.

8. Rack into glass.

9. Rack monthly until clear. (Note: If it is not clear in four months, add fining agent.)

10. Bottle; age 6–12 months.

Note: Many people use tart apples or crabapple/apple combinations. If, however, you choose to use apple cider, you *must* use freshly squeezed, totally unadulterated juice. The preservative gook that commercial juice guys flood bulk cider with will zap your yeast and, presto—no ferment-o!

HoneyHop Metheglin:
based on Jace's "Swamp Water Mead-Ale"
(Makes 1 gallon)

This recipe is satisfyingly fast and dramatic. It is a good recipe to use if you want to have something to sample while you wait patiently for that long-aging sack mead you've started. The hops add a nice bittering undertone to the sweet honey in the pot. However, be sure to use a robust fall honey that can hold its own against the hoary hop.

Ingredients

3   pounds Goldenrod/Aster (mixed fall wildflower) honey

1   ounce leaf hops

peel of half a lemon and half a lime; squeeze of juice from both

1   teaspoon yeast energizer

1   packet Montrachet yeast

Procedure

1. In an enamel pan, dissolve honey in 6 pints of water.

2. Put $^3/_4$ once of the leaf hops in a mesh bag and add to the mix.

3. Bring to just below boiling and hold there for an hour, skimming the froth as it rises.

4. Stir in yeast energizer, citrus peel and juice, and remaining $^1/_4$ once of leaf hops. Boil for an additional 5 minutes.

5. Remove from heat, cover, and let cool overnight.

6. Rack off the hops and other stuff into a plastic bucket.

7. Add enough good water to make 1 gallon and pitch in the yeast.

8. Skim foam daily.

9. When foam recedes, rack into a glass gallon jug, top up with sterilized water, and attach an air lock.

10. Rack off the sediment as needed.

11. Bottle when clear; age 6–9 months.

Howling Jack: Honey Pumpkin Mead
(Makes approximately 1 gallon)

This recipe was contributed by one of my all-time heroines, grand dame of fermentation, Grace Firth (see the Appendix for a listing of her books). The authentic country recipe and methodology will set some lab rats to squealing, no doubt, but others will have great fun with it. Grace reports that this mead is the color of a ripe peach and smells like autumn leaves.

Mead brewed in the pumpkin treats the pumpkin itself as the secondary fermenter. You can prepare your favorite mead recipe and when it comes time to rack into the secondary fermenter, rack into the prepared, plump pumpkin instead. You will need to seal the pumpkin body so it is air tight. Do this by means of a paraffin bath. Prepare a pumpkin as you would a jack o' lantern, cutting a top that will become the lid (make sure it seats snugly, leaving no gaping air holes), rip out the "guts"—seeds, membranes, monkey brains—and rinse with water. You might experiment with some other large bodied fruits and vegetables as well. honey-watermelon mead holds some intriguing possibilities. You might use the fruit pulp and juice and a lesser ammount of honey.

Ingredients

1   sound, large-bodied pumpkin—somewhere in the neighborhood of 1-gallon capacity (if you can't find a jumbo-plumpo boy, use two smaller 'kins and split the liquid between them.)

3   pounds fall wildflower honey

1 $^1/_2$ unpeeled citrus fruits—orange, lemon, lime, or any combination thereof—well-scrubbed and chopped coarsely

1   tablespoon strong black brewed tea

2   tablespoons bee pollen
     (alternative: 1 teaspoon yeast energizer)

1   package of wine yeast

     good water sufficent to make up 1 gallon total

Procedure

1. Prepare yeast starter.

2. Sterilize honey-water by boiling for 10 minutes, skimming the froth as it rises.

3. Remove pot from heat, stir in fruit, tea, yeast energizer. Allow to cool.

4. Pitch the yeast.

Prepare the Pumpkin

1. Cut the top off, carefully making sure it will re-seat securely.

2. Gut and clean it; rinse.

3. Fill a plastic bucket full of hot water. Melt the paraffin wax on the surface of the water.

4. Dip the pumpkin, bottom first, until it is coated *up to* the rim. (Do not get the wax inside.)

5. Remove the coated pumpkin and *quickly* pour your prepared recipe into the body cavity of Mr. Jack. Leave about an inch of air space between the liquid and the rim of the opening. Top with water if needed.

6. Replace the top. Seal the seam with melted paraffin.

7. Place in a quiet dark spot for about 2 months.

After two months, Grace suggests liberating the brew by breaking the seal and siphoning off into bottles. For you more cautious types, you might want to siphon off into a glass secondary, fit with an air lock for evaluation. If the fermentation is not complete and you bottle prematurely, the corks may blow and all your patient efforts will come to naught.

Other Drinks

Fire Dance Wassail: Party Bowl
(alcoholic or not; makes approximately 1 gallon)

Preparing the Apples

  6   medium tart apples

$1/4$ cup brown sugar

  1   teaspoon cinnamon

$1/8$ teaspoon grated lemon rind

Core the apples to within $1/4$ inch of the bottom. Mix the sugar and spices in a bowl and fill the empty core-space of the apples. Place the apples in a shallow pan with $3/4$ cup boiling water. Bake at 375 degrees until tender but not mushy (about 30 minutes).

Preparing the Wassail

1 gallon apple cider

6 baked apples and their juices (in a pinch, you can substitute canned baked apples)

1 teaspoon vanilla

2 sticks cinnamon

2 teaspoons whole cloves

1 whole nutmeg, cracked

3–4 pieces crystallized ginger, cut into small pieces

1 lemon rind

1. Pour cider into a large kettle. Add apples and spices.

2. Cover and bring slowly to a boil.

3. Simmer for about 5 minutes.

4. If the kettle is respectable, carry it directly to the table; if not, pour the brew into a heat-proof bowl and serve.

For Alcoholic Wassail Only

1 1/2–2 cups mead (if you drank all the mead already, substitute a light, sweet white wine)

2 cups bourbon, applejack, or cognac

Stir in the mead or wine. In a separate metal pan, slightly warm the bourbon. Now, dim the house lights, remove the liquor from the heat, and set it aflame with a long taper (a straw from a broomstick works well). Pour the flaming liquor into the wassail where it will ignite the bigger brew. Let the blue flames boogie briefly before dunking them into the drink with a ladle.

The Promise of Pomegranate Cordial
(Makes approximately 1 quart)

Like the apple, the pomegranate practically oozes mythical significance. The word comes from Middle French *pomme grenate*, which means, literally, "seedy apple." The pomegranate is a key element in the Persephone-Demeter story and has come to symbolize the eternal, female-specific energy of renewal and re-creation.

Ingredients

    4 1/2   cups pomegranate seeds (liberate them from the
            tough outer skin and membranes; mash coarsely)

    1/2   cup light honey

      3   cups generic vodka

Procedure

Place all ingredients in a tightly capped bottle and shake vigorously. Let sit in a darkened spot for at least 3 weeks, agitating the bottle periodically. Strain liquid off the fruit into decorative bottles. May be used as a cordial, dessert topping, or mixed with club soda as a spritzer.

Sneezy's Honey Mint Brandy
(Makes approximately 1 quart)

This flavored brandy is guaranteed to chase away your cold and sneezies or at least make them more tolerable. It is based on a traditional American colonial recipe.

Ingredients

2	cinnamon sticks
3	whole cloves
1	tablespoon raisins
$1/8$	teaspoon coarsely ground black pepper
1	tablespoon fresh ginger root, peeled and chopped
$1/2$	cup fresh mint leaves
1	quart inexpensive brandy
1 $1/2$	cup honey

Procedure

Put the first six ingredients into a clean, dry bottle with a tight-fitting lid. Add in the bandy, shake vigorously. Let the mixture steep in a darkened spot for about 10 days. Give the bottle a good shake every few days.

At the end of that time, filter the cordial into a clean bottle (use a funnel and a coffee filter), add the honey and shake some more. Let the brandy age for another 2–3 weeks, filter it again and rack out into decorative bottles. **Note:** This brandy often has a precipitate regardless of filtering. You can either live with it, or let the brandy "settle" and siphon the clear stuff off with a turkey baster (one you have bought specifically for the purpose).

Chapter 15

January Through April: Hibernation-Reawakening

IN THIS PART OF THE year, darkness prevails. In our times of uncertain faith, we often associate "darkness" with sinister, hopeless, or evil forces. In ritual making, however, we acknowledge the All, the ongoing, the eternal. The "dark time" that we celebrate, therefore, is the darkness before the dawn, a time of growing in the womb, dreaming of awakening in the sunlight.

Root vegetables, in particular, can be used to make robust meads for this chilly season. Because most vegetable meads are made from root vegetables, I have appropriated the Greek prefix *rhiz*, meaning *root*, to coin the term *rhizamel* for this category, to pay homage to this simple but honest ingredient.

Meads

The Veggies Will Rise Again Rhizamel
(Makes 3 gallons)

Preparing the Fortified Water

1   gallon total, root vegetables: parsnips, carrots,
    beets. Be sure to remove any green or rotten parts.

Scrub and chop the vegetables (don't peel them). Boil veggies
in 2 $^1/_2$ gallons of water until soft but not mushy. Let the brew
cool to room temperature, squeeze out the vegetables, and discard
(the vegetables, not the water).

The Rest of the Story

6   apples

3   potatoes

2   oranges

1 $^1/_2$ ounce ginger root

    handful raisins

$^1/_2$ cup prunes

5   pounds honey

    sherry yeast

    good water

1. Scrub, but don't peel, the first four ingredients.
   Chop them up and throw them into a primary
   plastic fermenter.

2. Add raisins, prunes, ginger root, honey, and vegetable water from Step 1.

3. Sterilize with $1/3$ teaspoon potassium metabisulphite (or 2 Campden tablets).

4. Let stand uncovered for 24 hours, then add the yeast. (You *did* make a yeast starter, didn't you?)

5. Let it work for 10 days–2 weeks, being sure to stir and smash the stew daily.

6. Strain the liquid off into a glass carboy or jug (discard the veggies and fruit). Allow the brew time to rest awhile and settle out.

7. After a day or two, rack off the sediment, top up with good water, attach air lock and allow the brew to complete fermentation.

8. When fermentation is complete and the brew has cleared, rack into bottles, and rave on.

Celtic Crusher Metheglin
(Makes 1 gallon)

Ingredients

    3   pounds dark, morose, and moody honey

$1/2$ ounce acid blend

       rind of one small lemon

    4 ounces mixed herbs (rosemary, marjoram, fennel, mace, camomile flowers—whatever smells good and is available)

handful of raisins

5   tablespoons bee pollen

darn good water, sufficient to make up a gallon
of liquid

Procedure

1. In a primary fermenter, stir the honey into 6 pints of
   the water.

2. Add in acid blend, lemon peel, bee pollen, raisins, and
   herbs (to make your life easier later: put the herbs in
   a cheesecloth bag first).

3. Sterilize with 2 Campden tablets or $1/3$ teaspoon
   potassium metabisulphite.

4. Let stand 24 hours.

5. Add in yeast starter and stand back.

6. After 4 days, take a tea strainer and fish out the herbs
   and other solid material. Skim scum daily.

7. After the foam recedes, rack into the secondary
   fermenter.

8. When fermentation is complete, rack into bottles and
   allow to age for at least a year.

Other Drinks

Lithuanian Krupnikas

(Spiced honey vodka; makes approximately 1 quart)

Ingredients

- 1/2 tablespoon caraway seeds
- 5 cloves
- 5 whole allspice
- 2 sticks cinnamon
- 1/2 nutmeg, cracked
- 2 strips orange rind
- 2 strips lemon rind
- 1 stick vanilla
- 2 pieces candied ginger
- pinch saffron
- 1/2 pound light honey
- 1 pint generic vodka
- 1 pint water (spring or bottled)

Procedure

1. Crack nutmeg and combine with other spices, fruit rind and water in an enamel or stainless steel pan.

2. Bring to a boil and maintain heat until the liquid is reduced to 1 cup.

3. Strain liquid off, using clean cheesecloth, into a heat-proof container.

4. Stir in honey and vodka, and mix well.

5. Cover and allow to cool completely.

6. Pour into a large, screw-top jar and let it sit for several weeks.

7. Siphon the liquor off the sediment and into decorative bottles.

Note: Krupnikas can be enjoyed straight up or mixed with milk and served over ice—a sweet combination of milk and honey.

Athole Brose
(Makes 1 pint)

A traditional Scottish Highland concoction, guaranteed to put a bloom on the cheek and weakness in the knee.

Ingredients

1   cup strong, dark honey

2   cups of whiskey (if you use Irish whiskey, you'll have to call it Athole Bruce)

sweet whipped cream

Procedure

Mix the honey and whiskey in a heat-proof pan and warm ever so slightly. Pour into mugs and top with sweet cream and a grating of nutmeg.

Noddin's Nightgown

For Children:

    1   cup hot milk

    1   teaspoon honey

For the Parents, add:

    1   shot of coffee liquor or dark rum

Procedure

Swirl together in a mug and send children (over the age of a year, please—milk and honey should not be given to infants) into dreamland. After they are asleep, make one for yourself, fortified with a jigger of coffee liquor or dark Jamaican rum, by gum.

Chapter 16

May Through August: Growth and Fruitfulness

SPRING AND SUMMER ARE FILLED with flowers and sweet, delicate fruit. Your early concoctions will, no doubt, feature spring flowers, from the roaring dandelion to the shy and shrinking violet; let your later summer fare be voluptuous, fragrant, riotous, and red.

Meads

DeNeenie's Dandelion Dragon (Metheglin)
(Makes 1 gallon)

Ingredients

2   quarts dandelion flowers

3   pounds honey

    peel of 1 whole lemon (or 1 teaspoon citric acid blend)

    juice of 1 orange

    handful of raisins

5   tablespoons bee pollen (or 1 teaspoon yeast nutrient)

1   tablespoon strong black brewed tea (or $1/4$ teaspoon tannin)

    champagne yeast

Procedure

1. Gather the flowers on a warm sunny day when the flowers are fully open. Pick off the petals and discard the green calyx and stem. Wash well to remove any persistent insects. Place in a large bowl, pour in a gallon of boiling water and stir. Allow to cool overnight.

2. When cool, strain the petals out of the water, and discard them.

3. Mix honey and flower water in the primary fermenter, along with the orange juice, lemon peel, pollen, raisins, and tea. (The traditional recipe does not call for it, but you may want to sterilize the honey-water mixture with with $1/3$ teaspoon of potassium metabisulfite. In this case, let stand 24 hours before pitching the yeast.)

4. Add in the yeast starter and swirl the whole mess to aerate.

5. Cover loosely, skim froth daily until the primary fermentation is complete and the foam begins to recede.

6. Rack into a secondary glass fermenter, top up with good spring water, and add an air lock.

7. Rack off the sediment every four weeks or so until the fermentation is complete.

8. Rack into bottles, age for at least a year.

Honeysuckle Heaven Metheglin
(Makes 1 gallon)

Ingredients

1   gallon honeysuckle flowers

2   cups light-colored raisins or sultanas

2   lemons, sliced

1   knob of ginger root, beaten and bruised

2 $1/2$ pounds light honey

champagne yeast

Procedure

1. Gather blooms when the sun has climbed high enough to dry the dewy tears from the cheek of the honeysuckle. Discard any stems, leaves, or calyx.

2. Cover blossoms with 2 gallons of boiling water and simmer for 20 minutes.

3. Strain out the blooms and discard.

4. Stir in honey, lemons, sultanas, and ginger root

5. Sterilize must with 2 crushed Camden tablets.

6. Let cool to room temperature

7. Add in yeast starter.

8. Skim must daily until foam recedes.

9. Rack into secondary fermenter.

10. When fermentation is complete and mead clears, rack into bottles and age for 6 months to a year.

Witch-Away Elderflower Mead
(Makes 5 gallons)

Elder flowers, Grace Firth tells us, have traditionally been used by gypsies as protection against "bad witches." If there is a bad witch casting about in your neighborhood, protect yourself with the powers of the elders. You can also make elderberry mead, but it is the flowers specifically that are believed to impart protection.

Ingredients

- $1/2$ bushel of elder flowers

- 15 pounds strong, fearless honey

- 1 $1/2$ pounds raisins

  peels of 3 lemons (alternate: 4 teaspoons acid blend)

  Montrachet yeast

Procedure

1. Pick the elder flowers after the sun has kissed them, and before the buggies have bitten them.

2. Wash, discard leaves, stems, and calyx.

3. Place elders in a heat-proof pot and cover with 5 gallons of boiling water.

4. Stir in honey, lemon peel, and raisins; cover and let cool overnight.

5. Next morning, stir in the yeast starter and let the brew ferment loosely covered, skimming daily for about a week.

6. Rack into the secondary fermenter fitted with an air lock.

7. Allow fermentation to complete and must to clear.

8. Rack into bottles and age at least 6 months. The "bouquet" of this mead, by the way, can be as strong as its powers.

Ravishing in Red: Raspberry Melomel
(Makes 3 gallons)

Ingredients

    10   pounds light honey

    $1/2$ cup raisins

         juice of 3 lemons

    1–2   pints of fresh raspberries

         champagne yeast

Procedure

1. Mash the raspberries coarsely in a bowl to break the skins. (You can either pour the fruit directly into the must or suspend the fruit in a cheesecloth bag.)

2. Mix all the ingredients (except the yeast) together and sterilize with $1/3$ teaspoon of sodium metabisulphite.

3. Let must sit overnight. Prepare the yeast starter.

4. Pitch the yeast.

5. Skim daily until the foam recedes.

6. Rack into the secondary fermentation container and fit with an air lock.

7. Ferment until clear.

8. Age 6 months.

Points to Remember

A. Boiling will set the fruit pectin, creating a haze that is all but impossible to get rid of. So, if you boil to sterilize, boil the honey-water first and then add the fruit.

B. Some melomel recipes call for retaining the fruit in the mixture beyond the primary fermentation stage. As long as you have fruit pulp or skins floating in the mix *you must use an open fermenter* (bucket loosely covered with cloth or plastic). Otherwise the gook can plug up the air lock and blow everything to kingdom come.

C. This recipe calls for a modest amount of fruit. I can personally vouch for it, having sipped it under the summer oaks at Mike's house. Other melomels call for mondo fruito: 2 pounds of fruit per gallon. Obviously, there is a lot of leeway. Let your taste buds lead you.

D. Substitute other berries: black or blueberry, elderberry, mulberry or strawberry, cranberry, or any combination thereof.

Traditional Ethiopian T'ej

T'ej is the traditional drink of Ethiopia. Women brewers have preserved the recipes and methods for generations. Traditional recipes do not call for the addition of a cultured wine yeast, but rather indulge the wild child, the naturally occuring osmophilic yeast found in honey. You can do the native thing—wild and unpredictable—or you can saunter safely with the European interloper *Saccharomyces cerviseae, ellipsoideus*.

Understand, further, that when Ethiopians gather wild honey, they gather the whole ball of wax—honeycomb, crushed larvae, pollen, trapped bees, all swimming to glory in a lake of golden honey. This is a truly "organic" forage crop which is traditionally brewed in the calabash, that great cosmic egg. Oftentimes a woman brewer will reserve a portion of the family's t'ej to seed the next batch. She may also secure some herbal material from the village "wise woman" to ensure a good ferment.

The brew is mixed up then left out in the sun to ferment. The intensity of the African sun gets the ingredients hopping and the t'ej is ripe and ready within a few hours. It is consumed while still actively fermenting as it will not keep for extended periods of time.

Traditional Recipe

1 part honey to 5 parts water (use honeycomb with brood, pollen, and honey still intact—crush and mix with water to the desired sweetness)

handful of dried Geisha or Gesho leaves for bittering (those in temperate regions may have to substitute woody hops)

beer yeast (if you don't have a "seed" ferment available)

Procedure

1. Mix everything up in a calabash gourd (or earthenware crock) and set in the summer sun for 5 days.

2. Remove Geisha or hops with a tea strainer.

3. Drink it up and boogie on down.

Note: Modern variations on this recipe include boiling the honey-water and hops; straining the hops after 5 days; then adding more ingredients. The doctored brew sits an additional 15–20 days and is stored in a cool place.

Suggestions for Additional Ingredients

medium citron—seedless, peeled, sliced

coffee beans—roasted

orange peels

ginger

prunes—1 pound/gallon

bananas—1 medium fruit/gallon

Other Drinks

Briz: Traditional Ethiopian Children's Drink
(Makes 1 $^{1}/2$ quarts)

Ingredients

$^{1}/2$ cup pure honey

6   cups of soda or spring water

juice of 1 lemon

Procedure
Stir together, set in a sunny window for 2 days. Refrigerate and add ice before serving. Garnish with a lime wheel.

Midsummer Mulberry Madness

An urban forager friend of mine depended on mulberries as her staple summer fruit. Most city people dislike mulberries and their messy purple splatterings, and are more than happy to have someone else gather them up and take them away.

Ingredients

    1   pound mulberries

    $3/4+$ cup honey

         juice of 2 lemons

         soda water or ginger ale

Procedure

1. Wash and de-stem berries.

2. Press fruit through a sieve then strain again, using cheesecloth.

3. Combine the mulberry juice, lemon juice, and honey. Adjust the sweetness according to taste.

4. Mix with soda water or ginger ale over ice.

5. Share drinks and poetry with your fellow foragers.

Part 4

Commercial Meadmaking

Chapter 17

Meadery
Madness

W̲HEN̲ I̲ STARTED THE A̲MERICAN Mead Association (AMA) in 1986, the term *meadery* was little more than a historical novelty. There were a couple of wineries that made honey wine, although few of them actually called it "mead." A notable exception was Camelot Mead, produced by Oliver Winery in Bloomington.

As more and more people became intrigued with mead and its commercial potential, however, the notion of meaderies, wineries that make mead exclusively, caught fire. In 1988, Bob Stevens, president of Betterbee, a beekeeping supply company, teamed up with meadmaking chemist Wayne Thygessen. Together they opened the first North American meadery: the Meadery at Greenwich. Since that historic moment, almost a dozen meaderies have either opened their doors or will do so in the near future. Additionally, a number of established wineries have added mead to their other fruit wine production.

During my years as director of the American Mead Association, I found myself in the position of working with many meadery people, helping to establish networks for technical and marketing support. I started a meadery myself, Dancing Bear, which unhappily did not survive infancy. I learned a lot from my own experience as well as from the experiences of those I worked with—what to do, what not to do, what we all might do differently the next time around.

If you are toying with the idea of going commercial with your meadmaking—and you can begin with as little as 300 gallons— keep in mind that there are three general aspects you will need to consider: legal, technical, and financial. They are all equally important. A deficiency in any one of these areas will cause you no end of trouble in the other two.

Legal: Paperwork, Paperwork, and More Paperwork

The very first thing you must reconcile yourself to, the moment you enter the commercial arena, is that you will spend many, many hours dealing with paperwork. Commercial wine production is controlled by the Federal Bureau of Alcohol, Tobacco and Firearms (BATF), which in turn is under the jurisdiction of the Treasury Department. Because it is a federal bureaucracy, the BATF is fueled by government forms—in triplicate. Add to that the requirements of state and local bureaucracies with their own forms and filing procedures and you'll understand something of the task that confronts you.

To manufacture and sell alcoholic beverages, you must first obtain the appropriate licenses and permits. You will need both a federal and state license. Get all the applications at the same time as you will find yourself constantly engaged in a Catch-22 situation: you must have permit A before you can apply for permit B. Applying for permit B is contingent on your having filed permit A, and so on. Contact your state liquor control board (check the phone book for information) first for state forms. At the same time, get the address of the regional BATF office where you can request federal forms.

When you get the applications, you will begin to get an inkling of what you are in for. I used to think people were kidding when they told me the completed application packet weighed three pounds. They weren't. It does.

Each state has its own regulations regarding the establishment of a commercial winery. There is no such designation as "meadery"; you are either a winery, brewery, or distillery. Breweries produce beers or ales containing up to 7 percent alcohol; wineries produce wines of 7 to 14 percent alcohol. To produce any beverage with a higher alcoholic percentage, including fortified wines, such as ports and sherries, requires a distillery license. Many micro-breweries are currently experimenting with mead-ale and honey beers. Be clear about the product you intend to manufacture. Don't tease and confuse the state employee by speaking about "brewing mead" when what you really mean is "making mead." I made this slip-up and the agent in charge was ready to make me file as a brewery because in his mind "brewing" obviously meant "brewery." The application fee for a winery at that time was $64 while a brewery application cost a whopping $3,000. Be precise; details count.

In addition, each county and township may have further restrictions as to where and how you may operate a winery. In some areas, you will find that the law prohibits establishment of any alcohol related business within a specific radius of a school, church, or senior citizen center. Other jurisdictions may be "dry" or have other prohibitions. Needless to say, it behooves you to find all of this out before you purchase a building or begin filing for a license.

Some states require that you procure a suitable building and have the necessary equipment in place before they will issue a permit to begin commercial production. You may not legally begin to make mead intended for commercial sale until you have been issued a commercial permit. Your personal backlog of aging mead cannot be sold commercially the week after you receive your permit.

Each state has its own regulations as to what ingredients it will allow in the production of an alcoholic beverage. Thus, that traditional mead recipe you have been using for years may not cut the mustard with the permit police. Further, there are differences in allowable ingredients between state and federal agencies. In case of discrepancy, the state regulation prevails. Save yourself a lot of time (which quickly translates into money) and a lot of frustration; know ahead of time what they allow and don't allow before submitting your recipe. If you are not sure, ask the state agent—he or she will be happy to tell you. Some people breeze right through this process with no problem. Then again, I recall talking with an experienced winery owner who had his mead recipes rejected repeatedly. It took him three years of revising and refiling until he came up with a mead recipe that made it through the approval process.

Recipes have to be approved, bottle labels have to be approved, physical facilities have to be approved, financing has to be approved, any winery workers have to be approved, and all these areas will involve filing mountains of paperwork. Be prepared for this aspect; it can literally make or break you. Meadmaker Khiron (As You Like It Meadery) found his training as an army clerk invaluable when it came to filing government forms. "I was a clerk, so I learned how the government likes to speak and hear things. I was perfectly confident that I could wade through the papers without a lawyer." If you do not have Khiron's ability or background, however, heed his advice and hook up with "someone who can read and write 'Governmentalese.'"

The prevailing wisdom in filing anything with a governmental agency is: color within the lines. Do nothing out of the ordinary that will call attention to your petition. Do nothing to cause a state or federal clerk to flag your file, to question, to hold up for further information, or to simply send the whole mess back to you with instructions to refile.

Do whatever it takes to get your license first. You can get experimental or radical after you are underway. One frustrated meadery owner who had been caught in a bureaucratic paper-swamp for three years was advised "off the record" to apply for a regular winery permit and then submit "honey-wine" as one of his recipes. Another winery owner told me he had dropped the name "mead" from his bottles, opting instead for the less controversial designation of honey-fruit wine. He said that the hassle simply wasn't worth it.

So, keep your nose clean and choose your battles wisely. Otherwise, you will find yourself sinking below the surface, awash in the sea of paperwork, before you ever get out of the harbor.

Technical: Equipment and Oenology

Meadmaking, although similar in many ways to grape winemaking, poses unique problems and challenges simply because honey does not behave like grapes in the fermentation process. The old bugaboo, clarification, can become a major problem in commercial production. While a home meadmaker with five gallons of cloudy mead is mildly inconvenienced, a commercial producer sitting on 500 gallons of stuck mead faces financial disaster. Some commercial meadmakers report that clarification has never been a problem for them; they sulfite, ferment, add fining agents and bottle. Others, however, have been less fortunate.

Over the past few years, researchers at Cornell University's Agricultural Research Station have ushered in a whole new era for commercial meadmaking based on ultrafiltration. Ultrafiltration is a process by which the honey is run through a series of perforated tubes housed in a stainless steel body. During this process, honey is filtered to such an fine degree that protein molecules, which can inhibit clarification, are removed. Thus, meadmaking, which until now required months, even years, to achieve a marketable product, now can be accomplished in a matter of weeks. Since you are required to pay taxes on inventory—the mead in process as well as the finished product—being able to turn the product around in a timely fashion has major financial implications.

Robert Kime and his associates were originally testing the ultrafiltration process unit for use in the fruit-juice industry. A call from a newly opened meadery, however, prompted Kime, a beekeeper and mead enthusiast himself, to consider ultrafiltration for commercial meadmaking. The results have been overwhelmingly positive. Ultrafiltration produces a light, crystal-clear mead with no objectionable taste whatsoever, and it does so in as short a period as ten days.

Nonetheless, it is a good news/bad news scenario. The bad news, as one might expect, is the cost of the units. At this writing, a new ultrafiltration unit costs between $15,000 and $200,000. Despite this sobering factor, three wineries in New York state and a newly opened meadery in Colorado have enthusiastically embraced this technological wonder worker.

Be assured that not everyone chooses this path. There are still commercial producers who opt for the "traditional" way of heating honey, or who are unruffled by a longer fermentation time. There are both aesthetic and financial considerations involved. Critics maintain that a lot of the distinctive characteristics of mead are lost through ultrafiltration, that the resulting mead tastes suspiciously like a Chardonnay wannabe. Your best source of information in considering all the options available is to talk to the people who actually make mead. The American Mead Association maintains a list of commercial mead producers, both domestic and worldwide (see Appendix for the AMA address). It is currently the only such listing available.

Commercial meadmaking has much in common with commercial winemaking. You can learn a great deal from attending wine or oenological workshops and conventions. Plug yourself into the winery network; as wineries upgrade and enlarge, they often sell off older or smaller equipment. You can save yourself a considerable amount of money by buying used equipment.

The professional winemaking industry relies on the services of oenologists, scientists who specialize in winemaking. Some states employ an oenologist in conjunction with the Cooperative Extension Service to assist wine makers. Since you are required to submit regular laboratory reports on your mead in progress, oenologists are valuable people to know. They can also help track down the latest research on many wine-related topics.

Be aware, however, that most funded research is sponsored by grape growers associations. Those growers understand the economic importance of the wine industry. A similar initiative has not surfaced among the honey producers, although perhaps this will change. The American Mead Association was started with the expressed purpose of creating an alternative market for honey. In an off-the-record conversation with a Honey Board official, however, I was told that the honey industry was reluctant to support any alcohol-related product. The majority opinion was that such support might compromise the "healthy" image that honey enjoys.

Financial: Money and Means

Make no mistake—commercial meadmaking is capital intensive. You will need substantial amounts of money "up front" to cover buildings, equipment, legal fees, and the many other expenses that will surface before you ever open the door. Additionally, you will probably need an independent source of income for the first year or so after your winery or meadery opens.

Unless you win the lottery or inherit a phenomenal amount of money, you will have to do some creative planning to make your dreams a reality. One of the most common and trustworthy avenues is to piggyback a meadery onto an existing business. The Meadery at Greenwich (now called Betterbee Meadery), for instance, is part of Bob Stevens' Betterbee bee-supply business. Khiron, along with other members of his intentional community, expanded a Massachusetts main street bakery, As You Like It,

into a meadery as well. Several honey farms, California's Hon-
eyRun and Idaho's Life Force, for instance, invested part of their
inventory into a meadmaking enterprise.

Although most of the wine research grants are sponsored by
grape growers, there are other operating grants available if you
are willing to dig. The Betterbee people were awarded a sizable
agricultural grant when they were able to demonstrate that the
state beekeeping industry stood to profit from their meadery. In
my own case, I was awarded a New Woman-New Business grant
from *New Woman* magazine for my meadery, based (among other
things) on the fact that it was a woman-owned, environmentally
sound business.

Keep in mind that honey is earth-friendly; it is a forage crop
that does not impact negatively on the environment. Vineyards
require massive amounts of irrigation in some areas; honey does
not. Honeybees provide a valuable agricultural service—pollination. Honey is a beneficial by-product for that activity. When you
are considering grants, therefore, think rural rehabilitation, land
use, sustainable agriculture, and appropriate technology.

Meadmaking may also become inheritor of a very old tradition, taking up where "spirited" monks have left off. Khiron and
company run their meadery as an economic extension of their
intentional, spiritually based community. In another such
instance, a group of Hindu monks I spoke with were considering
expanding their apiary, honey-bakery business to include mead.
Mead, with its sacred associations for many different religious
and ethnic groups, has the potential for becoming the economic
backbone for many spiritual and cooperative communities.

Appendix

Resources for Meadmakers

Beekeeping

THERE ARE A ZILLION GOOD books and instructional videos about beekeeping. Some of the suppliers listed below offer an extensive array of choices. To find beekeeping groups in your area, contact your state Agriculture Department or the local office of the Cooperative Extension Service.

A. I. Root Co.
623 W. Liberty St.
Medina, OH 44256
1-800-289-7668

Beekeeping supplies; publisher of *Gleanings in Bee Culture*, magazine for beekeepers of all levels; good source of books and equipment.

Dadant & Sons
51 S. 2nd. St.
Hamilton, IL 62341
(217) 847-3324; Fax: 217-847-3660

Beekeeping supplies; publisher of *American Beekeeping Journal*.

Brushy Mountain Bee Farm
Rt. 1 Box 135
Moravian Falls, NC 28654
1-800-BEESWAX

Beekeeping supplies, gifts, books, videos. Meadmaking kits; producer of the *Magic of Mead* video.

Beekeeping Education Service/Wicwas Press
P.O. Box 817
Cheshire, CT 06410-0817
(203) 250-7575 (number is also a fax line)

Publisher of *BeeScience*; extensive catalog of bee, mead books, videos and teaching aids.

Commercial Beekeeping

Agricultural Technical Institute
Ohio State University
Wooster, OH
(216) 263-3684; Fax: 216-262-2720

Dr. James Tew and his lively crew offer the only U.S. program in commercial beekeeping.

Meadmaking

American Mead Association
P.O. Box 4666
Grand Junction, CO 81502
1-800-639-MEAD

Publishers of *Meadmakers Journal*; sponsor of Ambrosia Adventure Mead Only Competition; supplier of books, meadery directory, and meadmaking supplies.

American Homebrewers Association
P.O. Box 287
Boulder, CO 80306-0287

Publisher of *Zymurgy* magazine; clearinghouse of brewing information; sponsors annual conference, competition for home-brewers, which includes mead categories.

Mazer Cup Mead Competition
Ken Schramm
8740 Harding
Taylor, MI 48180

Annual mead competition with seven categories.

The Beverage People
Byron Burch
840 Piner Road #14
Santa Rosa, CA 95403
For advice call: (707) 544-2520; to place orders: 1-800-544-1867

Source of wine, mead, and beer making supplies, including a mead-specific nutrient blend; publisher of the *Beverage People News* which often includes mead recipes; books, advice line.

Other Competitions

Many state fairs have wine competitions, often including a "novelty" or other-than-grape category; some beekeeping associations, including the Eastern Apicultural Society, have honey shows that include a mead category. Also wine organizations such as the American Wine Society (3006 Latta Road, Rochester, NY 14612) have competitions that may include mead. These "special interest" group competitions, however, are usually restricted to members of the organization.

Books

Making Mead (Honey Wine) by Roger Morse, WicWas Press, Ithaca, NY 1980.

Making Mead by Bryan Acton and Peter Duncan, Amateur Winemaker Publications, Herts, England, 1984.

Brewing Mead/Wassail! In Mazers of Mead by Lt. Col. Robert Gayre with Charlie Papazian (reissue of 1948 classic), Brewers Publications, Boulder, CO, 1986.

All About Mead by S. W. Andrews, Northern Bee Books, West Yorkshire, England, 1982.

Honey Wines and Beers by Clara Furness, Northern Bee Books, West Yorkshire, U.K.

Mead Making Handbook (second edition) by Jace Crouch and Mike Murray, Asatru Alliance, Payson, AZ, 1989.

A Natural Year by Grace Firth, Simon & Schuster, 1972.

Secrets of the Still by Grace Firth, EPM, 1983.

Stillroom Cookery by Grace Firth, EPM, 1977.

All of Grace Firth's books are recommended. (Unfortunately, the first two listed titles are out of print. Check libraries, used book stores, et cetera.)

The Homebrewer's Guide to Meadmaking by Dave Suda. Recently published. Contact him by e-mail at suda@vrg.toronto.edu or by regular mail at 161 Viewmount Ave. Toronto, ON M6B IT5 Canada.

Other Books of Related Interest

Honey—A Comprehensive Survey, Eva Crane, ed. Published in cooperation with the International Bee Research Association.

The Sacred Bee by Hilda Ransome, reprinted by Bee Books Old and New.

The Bees of Buckfast Abbey by Brother Adam, published by British Bee Publications.

The Closet of Sir Kenelm Digby Knight Opened (1669), Anne MacDonell, ed., 1910. Published by Philip Lee Warner.

The War of the Gods: The Social Code in Indo-European Mythology by Jarich G. Oosten, published by Routledge & Kegan Paul.

Super Formulas: How to Make More Than 360 Useful Products That Contain Honey and Beeswax by Elaine C. White, published by Valley Hills Press (Starkville, MS).

A Country Year: Living the Questions by Sue Hubbell, published by Random House.

(See the Bibliography for specific additional publication information on these books.)

Herbs

Herb Research Foundation
1007 Pearl St. Ste. 200F
Boulder, CO 80302

These folks publish a version of the FDA's GRAS (Generally Recognized As Safe) listing, which is a compilation of botanicals that can be safely added to foods. If you are experimenting with metheglins, you might want to get a copy of this list to avoid problems and get some additional ideas.

Notes

Part 1: Milk and Honey in Myth and Ritual

Chapter 1: Background: Milk and Honey as Godstuff

1. Hilda M. Ransome. *The Sacred Bee* (Burrowbridge: BBNO, reprinted 1986; orig. 1937), 183.

This is an amazing compendium of information about the sacred associations and traditions of people world-wide when it comes to bees and their products. Written by anthropologist Ransome in 1937, it still stands as a primary text about the relationship of human and bee.

2. Ibid., 224.

3. Ibid., 251.

4. Ibid., 196.

5. Esther Peck. *National Costumes of the Slavic Peoples* (New York: The Womans Press, 1920), 2.

Chapter 2: Birth and Baptism Rituals

1. Photina, "Honey," an unpuplished paper by a Bene- dictine nun in Germany, written at an unknown date. This paper contains a wealth of information about pagan practices as well as a Christian theological con- sideration of honey.

2. Ransome, op. cit., 278.

3. Ibid., 280.

Chapter 3: Puberty Rituals

1. Juan Jose Arreola, *Confabulario and Other Inventions*. Trans. George Schade (Austin: UT Press, 1964), 178.

2. David Rockwell, *Giving Voice to Bear* (Niwot: Roberts Rinehart, 1991), 196. Anthropologist David Rock- well's book concentrates mainly on Native American beliefs and rituals dealing with bears. He does include some cross-cultural refererences, however, which show some interesting parallels in symbols and rituals. The honeybee is not native to the North American continent and was imported by Europeans in the 1600s. Native Americans refered to the honeybee as the white man's fly. There were however, other types

of bees indiginous to the Americas (see Levi-Strauss's *From Honey to Ashes*), but these bees did not produce honey in commercially viable ammounts as did the European honey bee.

3. Arreola, op. cit., 178.

4. Cameron, "A Bear Story." The poem itself can be found anthologized in *Touching Fire: Erotic Writings by Women* or in Cameron's book, *The Annie Poems*.

5. Rockwell, op. cit. 188.

6. Robert Gayre with Charlie Papazian, *Brewing Mead /Wassail! In Mazers of Mead* (Boulder, CO: Brewer's Publications, reprinted, 1986; orig. 1948), 22. This classic history of mead, first published in 1948, now updated with additions by American Homebrew Guru Charlie Papazian, still stands as one of the most comprehensive studies of mead tradition among the Aryan peoples. Be warned, however, that it is a product of the times and contains some offensive references to non-Aryan peoples.

7. Rockwell, op. cit., 10.

8. Ransome, op. cit., 290.

9. Gayre, op. cit. 24–25.

10. C. S. Lewis, *Surprised by Joy* (New York: Harcourt, Brace & World, Inc., 1955), 8.

Chapter 4: Marriage Rituals

1. Claude Levi-Strauss. *From Honey to Ashes* (New York: Harper & Row, translated 1973, orig. 1966), 143–145.

2. Ransome, op. cit., 179.

3. Ibid.

4. Virginia Davis, "T'ej in America," *Meadmakers' Journal* (1988). Davis did her research for this article in the Washington, D.C. area, which enjoys a substantial Ethiopian population. The immigrants sorely missed their native t'ej and approached Anthony Aellen, winemaker at Maryland's Berrywine Plantation. Aellen, who had been making a Medieval English style mead at the winery for nine years, agreed to undertake the task. The winery is still the only U.S. producer of t'ej to my knowledge.

5. Ransome, op. cit., 32.

6. An untitled poem by Psyche Torak (previously unpublished). Reprinted with permission.

7. Michael Sisson, "The Meadbearers of Odin," *American Meadmaker* (Vol. 1, No. 4, 1987).

Chapter 5: Death Rituals

1. Leonard J. Biallas, *Myths: Gods, Heroes and Saviors* (Mystic: Twenty-Third Publications, 1991), 246.

2. Michael Sisson, "Mead and the Ancient Celts," *Meadmakers' Journal* (1988).

3. Ibid.

4. Ransome, op. cit., 32.

5. Peck, op. cit., 2.

6. Homer, *The Odyssey*, trans. W. H. D. Rouse (New York: Mentor, 1937), 124.

Part 2: Making Mead

Chapter 7: Meadmaking: A User-Friendly Overview

1. Ken Schramm and Dan McConnell, "Minimum Conditions Required to Kill Yeasts in Honey," *Inside Mead* (Vol. 10, No. 1, June 1995), 23.

2. Ibid.

3. Clara Furness, *Honey Wines and Beers* (Hebden Bridge: Northern Bee Books, n.d.), 10.

4. Roger A. Morse, *Making Mead* (Ithaca, NY: Wicwas, 1980), 50–51. Dr. Morse, a distinguished professor of apiculture at Cornell University for many years, chose commercial meadmaking as the topic of his master's thesis. This is probably still the best resource available for the serious meadmaker.

Glossary

acid: a class of sour tasting substances used by meadmakers to balance the sweetness of the honey. Can be derived from natural sources, such as citrus fruits, or from a powdered concentrate that typically contains a combination of citric, mallic, and tartaric acids.

In sensory evaluation of wine and mead, acid refers to a sour, green taste that stimulates saliva—the mouth waters.

aerobic: activity that requires the presence of oxygen. Primary fermentation is aerobic.

additives: materials added to the must to enhance fermentation process.

adjuncts: materials added to the must to enhance the flavor of the finished mead.

air lock (fermentation lock, bubbler)**:** water-filled device fitted into a rubber stopper of the fermenter, and acts as a barrier to oxygen and a gate for escaping carbon dioxide.

anaerobic: activity accomplished in the absence of oxygen. Secondary fermentation is anaerobic.

apiculture: beekeeping.

BATF: Bureau of Alcohol, Tobacco and Firearms. Federal bureau that, among other things, licenses and controls the establishment and operation of commercial wineries.

brackett: see *mead variations*.

brew: (verb) originally understood to mean "to burn" or to make with fire or other heat source. Now can mean "mix together or combine."

carboy: big, glass container that holds the must; usually understood to hold three to five gallons.

cyser: see *mead variations*.

fermentation: transformation of a sugar source (honey) into alcohol and carbon dioxide through the activity of the yeast organism.

> **primary fermentation:** initial vigorous activity when the yeast is first introduced into the diluted sugar source. Because oxygen is required to initiate this activity, it is aerobic.

secondary fermentation: subsequent, less vigorous stage of fermentation that continues until all the available sugar has been converted to alcohol. Because this activity takes place in the absence of oxygen, it is anaerobic.

Secondary fermentation can also refer to fermentation that re-starts after all other visible indications of fermentation have ceased. Thus, we speak of secondary fermentation taking place in a quietly bottled mead that suddenly, inexplicably, blows its top.

"stuck" fermentation: incomplete fermentation.

fermenter: container in which the fermentation takes place.

open fermenter: container that allows the must contact with the air during the initial (primary) stage of fermentation. Can be a bucket or plastic trash can, for instance.

closed fermenter: container that prohibits contact between the must and surrounding air. Can be a stoppered carboy fitted with a water-filled fermentation lock, for instance.

primary fermenter: container in which the initial, vigorous fermentation takes place. May be open or closed.

secondary fermenter: container in which the subsequent fermentation takes place. Usually closed.

filtration: use of a filter or screen to physically remove contaminants in the honey or mead. Currently technology includes micro- and ultrafiltration processes.

fining agent: material added to a cloudy mead to bind the protein molecules and drags them out of suspension.

gruit: a mixture of herbs and spices used in the production of metheglin.

hydromel: see *mead variations*.

hydrometer: a device used to measure the sugar concentration of the must and thus project the expected alcohol concentration of the finished mead.

inoculating the must: see *pitching the yeast*.

lees: see *sediment*.

mazer: traditional drinking vessel for mead.

mead: alcoholic beverage that uses honey as its primary fermenting sugar source.

meaderie or meadery: a commercial winery that produces mead either exclusively or primarily.

mead variations: mead made with traditionally established additives, such as:

- Melomel (made by adding fruit).
- Metheglin (herbs and spices).
- Rhizamel (vegetables).

May also include specific variations:

- **Pyment** (grapes).
- **Morat** (mulberries).
- **Brackett** (malt).
- **Cyser** (apples and/or pears).
- **Rhodamel** (rose petals).
- **Hydromel** (watered mead).

melomel: see *mead variations.*

metheglin: see *mead variations.*

morat: see *mead variations.*

must: fermenting liquid; honey-water plus yeast and any additives or adjuncts.

oenologist: scientist who specializes in winemaking.

osmophilic: see *yeasts; osmophilic yeast.*

pitching the yeast (inoculating the must): introducing the yeast culture into the prepared must.

primary fermentation: see *fermentation; primary fermentation.*

pyment: see *mead variations.*

racking: process by which the must is siphoned off the sediment.

rhizamel: see *mead variations.*

rhodamel: see *mead variations.*

secondary fermentation: see *fermentation; secondary fermentation.*

sediment (lees): solid material that settles on the bottom of the container during fermentation; composed of dead yeast cells and other extraneous materials (bee legs, protein molecules, et cetera) settling out of suspension.

sensory evaluation: critical consideration of mead by means of the appropriate human senses of sight, taste, and smell.

"stuck" fermentation: see *fermentation; "stuck" fermentation.*

sulfites: sterilizing agent added to the must to kill off microorganisms through the action of sulfur dioxide. Examples: sodium metabisulphite, Campden tablets.

tannin: a substance often used in meadmaking that imparts an astringency, a mouth-drying sensation. Tannin binds proteins in solution and causes them to settle out as sediment, hence aiding in the clarifying process. It can be derived from natural sources, such as black tea, fruit skins, or bark, or is available in powdered form from winemaking suppliers.

yeasts: *Saccharomyces cerviseae*; one-celled organisms used in fermentation to convert sugars into alcohol.

> *ellipsoideus*: a variety of yeast suitable for winemaking. Gives optimum results because it will continue to ferment in higher alcohol concentrations, up to 12 to 18 percent alcohol.

osmophilic yeasts: so-called "wild yeast" found in honey; cannot survive in solutions of less than 30 percent sugar.

yeast energizer: nutrients added to the must to feed the yeast and keep it working; may be a commercial blend containing vitamins and minerals or derived from natural sources like raisins or bee pollen.

Bibliography

Books

Amerine, Maynard A. and Edward B. Roessler. *Wines: Their Sensory Evaluation*. San Francisco: W. H. Freeman & Co., 1976.

Acton, Bryan and Peter Duncan. *Making Mead*. Andover: Amateur Winemaker, 1968.

Andrews, S.W. *All About Mead*. Hebden Bridge, U.K.: Northern Bee Books, 1982.

Arreola, Juan Jose. *Confabulario and Other Inventions*. Trans. George Schade. Austin, TX: UT Press, 1964.

Berger, Pamela. *The Goddess Obscured*. Boston: Beacon Press, 1985.

Biallas, Leonard J. *Myths: Gods, Heroes and Saviors*. Mystic, CT: Twenty-Third Publications, 1991.

Bulfinch, Thomas. *Bullfinch's Mythology*. New York: Random House.

Calasso, Roberto. *The Marriage of Cadmus and Harmony*. New York: Alfred A. Knopf, 1993.

Crane, Eva, ed. *Honey: A Comprehensive Survey*. London: Heinemann, 1975.

Crouch, Jace and Mike Murray. *Mead Making Handbook*. Alma, MI: The Brewer's Guild, 1988.

Dailey, Sheila. *Bee Lore*. Mt. Pleasant, MI: Rumplestiltskin, 1986.

Firth, Grace. *A Natural Year*. New York: Simon & Schuster, 1972.

———. *Secrets of the Still*. McLean, VA: EPM Publications, Inc., 1983.

———. *Stillroom Cookery*. McLean, VA: EPM Publications, Inc., 1977.

Furness, Clara. *Honey Wines and Beers*. Hebden Bridge, U.K.: Northern Bee Books, n.d.

Gayre, Robert with Charlie Papazian. *Brewing Mead /Wassail! In Mazers of Mead*. Boulder, CO: Brewer's Publications, reprinted, 1986; orig. 1948.

Graves, Robert. *The White Goddess*. New York: Farrar, Straus and Giroux, 1948.

Homer. *The Odyssey*. Trans. W. H. D. Rouse. New York: Mentor, 1937.

Howe, George and G. A. Harrer. *A Handbook of Classical Mythology*. New York: F. S. Crofts & Co., 1929.

Kerenyi, Karl. *The Gods of the Greeks*. New York: Thames and Hudson, reprint, 1992; orig. 1951.

Larrington, Carolyne, ed. *The Feminist Companion to Mythology*. London: Pandora, 1992.

Lewis, C. S. *Surprised by Joy*. New York: Harcourt, Brace & World, Inc., 1955.

Levi-Strauss, Claude. *From Honey to Ashes*. New York: Harper & Row, translated 1973, orig. 1966.

McKenna, Terence. *Food of the Gods: The Search for the Original Tree of Knowledge*. New York: Bantam, 1972.

Morse, Roger A. *Making Mead*. Ithaca, NY: Wicwas, 1980.

Norman, Jill. *Honey*. New York: Bantam, 1991.

Oosten, Jarich G. *The War of the Gods: The Social Code in Indo-European Mythology*. London: Routledge & Kegan Paul, 1985.

Peck, Esther. *National Costumes of the Slavic Peoples*. New York: The Woman's Press, 1920.

Phillips, J. A. *Eve: The History of an Idea*. San Francisco: Harper & Row, 1984.

Ransome, Hilda M. *The Sacred Bee*. Burrowbridge, U.K.: BBNO, reprinted 1986; orig. 1937.

Rockwell, David. *Giving Voice to Bear*. Niwot, CO: Roberts Rinehart, 1991.

Rohde, Eleanour Sinclair. *Rose Recipes from Olden Times*. New York: Dover, reprinted 1973; orig. 1939.

Scott, Amoret. *A Murmur of Bees*. Oxford: Oxford Press, 1980.

Sibley, Jane. *The CA Guide to Brewing*. Milpitas, CA: Society for Creative Anachronism,1990.

Sperling, Les. *A Home Winemaker's Guide to Making Wine from Fruits*. Rochester, NY: American Wine Society, 1993.

Thornton, Sumrall, and Sturtevant, eds. *Touching Fire: Erotic Writings by Women*. New York: Carroll & Graf Publishers, Inc., 1989.

Articles

Davis, Virginia. "T'ej in America," *Meadmakers' Journal*, 1988.

Photina RECH. "Honey." (Unpublished paper; unspecified date) Holy Cross Abbey, Herstell, W. Germany.

Schramm, Ken and Dan McConnell. "Minimum Conditions Required to Kill Yeasts in Honey," *Inside Mead*, Vol. 10, No. 1, June 1995.

Sisson, Michael. "Earliest American Meads," *American Meadmaker*, Vol. 2, No. 2. 1987.

———. "Mead and the Ancient Celts," *Meadmakers' Journal*, 1988.

———. "The Meadbearers of Odin," *American Meadmaker*, Vol. 1, No. 4, 1987.

Index

Stay in Touch...

Llewellyn publishes hundreds of books on your favorite subjects.

On the following pages you will find listed some books now available on related subjects. Your local bookstore stocks most of these and will stock new Llewellyn titles as they become available. We urge your patronage.

Order by Phone

Call toll-free within the U.S. and Canada, **1–800–THE MOON**.
In Minnesota call **(612) 291–1970**.
We accept Visa, MasterCard, and American Express.

Order by Mail

Send the full price of your order (MN residents add 7% sales tax) in U.S. funds to:

> **Llewellyn Worldwide**
> **P.O. Box 64383, Dept. K683-1**
> **St. Paul, MN 55164–0383, U.S.A.**

Postage and Handling

- $4.00 for orders $15.00 and under
- $5.00 for orders over $15.00
- No charge for orders over $100.00

We ship UPS in the continental United States. We cannot ship to P.O. boxes. Orders shipped to Alaska, Hawaii, Canada, Mexico, and Puerto Rico will be sent first-class mail.

International orders: Airmail—add freight equal to price of each book to the total price of order, plus $5.00 for each non-book item (audiotapes, etc.); Surface mail—add $1.00 per item.

Allow 4–6 weeks delivery on all orders. Postage and handling rates subject to change.

Group Discounts

We offer a 20% quantity discount to group leaders or agents. You must order a minimum of 5 copies of the same book to get our special quantity price.

Free Catalog

Get a free copy of our color catalog, *New Worlds of Mind and Spirit*. Subscribe for just $10.00 in the United States and Canada ($20.00 overseas, first-class mail). Many bookstores carry *New Worlds*—ask for it!

Llewellyn's 1998 Magical Almanac

This beautifully illustrated almanac explores traditional earth religions and folklore while focusing on magical myths. Each month is summarized in a two-page format with information that includes the phases of the moon, festivals, and rites for the month, as well as detailed magical advice. This is an indispensable guide is for anyone who is interested in planning rituals, spells and other magical advice. It features writing by some of the most prominent authors in the field.

1-56718-935-0,
approx. 384 pp., 5 ^{3}/16 x 8, illus., softcover   **$6.95**

To order, call 1–800 THE MOON

192

The Complete Book of Incense, Oils and Brews

Scott Cunningham

For centuries the composition of incenses, the blending of oils, and the mixing of herbs have been used by people to create positive changes in their lives. With this book, the curtains of secrecy have been drawn back, providing you with practical, easy-to-understand information that will allow you to practice these methods of magical cookery.

Scott Cunningham, world-famous expert on magical herbalism, first published *The Magic of Incense, Oils and Brews* in 1986. *The Complete Book of Incense, Oils and Brews* is a revised and expanded version of that book. Scott took readers' suggestions from the first edition and added more than 100 new formulas. Every page has been clarified and rewritten, and new chapters have been added.

There is no special, costly equipment to buy, and ingredients are usually easy to find. The book includes detailed information on a wide variety of herbs, sources for purchasing ingredients, substitutions for hard-to-find herbs, a glossary, and a chapter on creating your own magical recipes.

0-87542-128-8, 288 pp., 6 x 9, illus., softcover $12.95

To order, call 1–800 THE MOON

A Kitchen Witch's Cookbook

Patricia Telesco

Appetizers • Breads • Brews • Canning & Preserving • Cheese & Eggs• Desserts • Meats • Pasta & Sauces• Quarter Quickies • Salads, Dressings & Soups • Tofu, Rice & Side Dishes • Vegetables• Witches' Dishes

Discover the joys of creative kitchen magic! *A Kitchen Witch's Cookbook* is a unique blend of tasty recipes, humor, history and practical magical techniques that will show you how cooking can reflect your spiritual beliefs as well as delightfully appease your hunger!

The first part of this book gives you techniques for preparing and presenting food enriched by magic. The second section is brimming with 346 recipes from around the world—appetizers, salads, beverages, meats, soups, desserts, even "Witches' Dishes"—with ingredients, directions, magical associations, history/lore and suggested celebrations where you can serve the food. (Blank pages at the end of each section encourage you to record your own treasured recipes.)

A Kitchen Witch's Cookbook makes it clear how ingredients found in any pantry can be transformed into delicious and magical meals for your home and circle, no matter what your path. Let Patricia Telesco show you how kitchen magic can blend your spiritual beliefs into delectable sustenance for both body and soul!

1-56718-707-2, 7 x 10 • 320 pp., illus., softcover $16.95

To order, call 1–800 THE MOON

Mother Nature's Herbal

Judith Griffin, Ph.D.

A Zuni American Indian swallows the juice of goldenrod flowers to ease his sore throat ... an East Indian housewife uses the hot spices of curry to destroy parasites ... an early American settler rubs fresh strawberry juice on her teeth to remove tartar. People throughout the centuries have enjoyed a special relationship with Nature and her many gifts. Now, with *Mother Nature's Herbal*, you can discover how to use a planet full of medicinal and culinary herbs through more than 200 recipes and tonics. Explore the cuisine, beauty secrets and folk remedies of China, the Mediterranean, South America, India, Africa and North America. The book will also teach you the specific uses of flower essences, chakra balancing, aromatherapy, essential oils, companion planting, organic gardening and theme garden designs.

1-56718-340-9,
7 x 10, 448 pp., 16-pg. color insert, softcover $19.95

To order, call 1–800 THE MOON

196

Designed and typeset by Amy Rost in Esprit with Party script.

Illustrations by Kathy Kruger.

Printed by Banta Information Services, Eden Prairie, Minnesota, on 45-lb. Mando Supreme paper.